Praise for TOMORROW | TODAY

At Salesforce, we're making the journey to AI easy for our customers—and Altify's AI solutions, built on the Salesforce platform, are a great example of our ecosystem at work. **TOMORROW | TODAY** is a guide for that journey, full of practical insight and perspective.

Todd Surdey, SVP, ISV and Channel Sales, Salesforce

With remarkable insight, **TOMORROW | TODAY** explains the profound technology and ethical impacts of AI on the future of sales, marketing and general business. Whether AI scares you or not, this thought provoking, but easily accessible, book will help you to predict how AI will impact your future.

Mark Roberge, Senior Lecturer, Harvard Business School; former CRO, Hubspot

Artificial and Augmented Intelligence is rapidly changing the leverage points in our lives: personally and professionally. **TOMORROW | TODAY** does a masterful job of helping us understand the journey we are on and will help us plot a course to a more efficient future.

Glenn Davis, Senior Vice President, Growth Execution and Client Engagement, Optum

A book full of insight and pragmatic thinking about what AI means for day-to-day workers. It's about the complete experience. When it comes to the right blend of humans and machines, **TOMORROW | TODAY** nails it.

Nick Mehta, CEO, Gainsight

Searching for a competitive advantage and mindful of mass disruption, board rooms have rushed to AI as the next big thing. The investments in AI pilots have moved from science projects to new digital business models powered by smart services. As clearly explained in Donal's book, the unifying force for digital transformation in customer journeys, IoT, future of work, commerce, and block chain technology is AI-driven smart services. Reading this book will help you understand why the shift from analytical systems to augmented humanity will have a profound impact on the world.

R "Ray" Wang, Principal Analyst and Founder, Constellation Research, Inc.

If history teaches one thing, it is that today's breathless technology headlines are tomorrow's punchlines. AI will change work, but not on its own. Ultimately organizations and people will change work as they incorporate AI into operations and strategy, and change processes to reflect these new tools. With deep insight into AI's interaction with professional work, Donal's book will help catalyze leading-edge thinking and serve as an impetus for innovative and practical business strategy.

Tom Monahan, Chairman and CEO, CEB (NYSE: CEB)

Artificial Intelligence has been the subject of debate and discussion for many years. Now it is becoming a reality. Not only has Donal Daly managed to explain it but, with his thinking on Augmented Intelligence, has taken it to a practical level that takes it from debate to useful. AI is now part of our lives. I'd make this book part of yours.

Paul Greenberg, author, CRM at the *Speed of Light* (4th edition), upcoming *The Commonwealth of Self Interest* (Harvard Business Publishing, 2017)

We have from day one believed that data and science are the keys to unlocking human potential. In a refreshingly clear manner, Donal captures the key trends and technology advances that are now actually enabling this in our day to day reality, as we enter the next era of technology-enabled performance, and **TOMORROW | TODAY** is a really good read.

Dave Elkington, Founder and CEO, Insidesales.com

Applications leveraging Augmented Intelligence transform the way humans make complex business decisions within the enterprise. **TOMORROW | TODAY** contains fascinating real world examples and thought-provoking narratives around the symbiotic relationship between man and machine. A valuable read.

Len Ferrington, Managing Director, Summit Partners

Donal is asking (and answering) the fundamental question: *"As machines get smarter, will humans continue to grow and ask the important questions?"* Artificial Intelligence is everywhere. If you want to understand what it means to you, you should read this book.

Ciaran Dynes, VP Products, Talend

TOMORROW | TODAY is a witty, illuminating and very readable guide to the rather complex of world of Artificial and Augmented intelligence. In Donal Daly's hands the subject is brought into focus, with telling observations and informative insights. This is a concise, but immensely useful and enjoyable book for anyone interested in the direction of new technologies and new generations of users.

Donald Farmer, Principal, TreeHive Strategy LLC

TOMORROW | TODAY is an outstanding investigation into how technology affects our workplace today and will influence how we work tomorrow. The narrative of the role Salesforce is playing in Augmented Intelligence is fascinating. Donal's book is informative, entertaining, straight to the point and a very important read for all sales and marketing professionals.

Daniel P. Strunk, Managing Director, Center for Sales Leadership, DePaul University

What generative design is to the future of making things, Augmented Intelligence is the information currency for the future of selling things; Donal expertly guides us to explore, and ultimately embrace, the possibilities of AI where the human is at the center and Augmented Intelligence is the ultimate Executive Assistant.

Julie Sokley, VP Global Sales Operations, Autodesk

TOMORROW | TODAY allows us to pause and think—a rare opportunity in today's noisy market. It draws our attention to how the new idea of 'augmenting intelligence' can help us go beyond just understanding data, to taking meaningful actions to improve our businesses, and ultimately, our lives.

Umberto Milletti, CEO and Founder, InsideView

TOMORROW | TODAY took me on a wonderful journey of fascinating content and profound insight. Donal translates a difficult topic into valuable, connected and important questions. The book is visionary and a 'must read' for business leaders who care about the future of man and machine.

Ingrid De Doncker, CEO, IDDConsult

The explosive growth of information gives rise to a fundamental truth: no human can process it all or should even try. Yet wise decisions must still be made in a world where Big Data is the new normal. That's why Donal Daly's new book is a 'must read' for leaders who wish to understand how computer-based intelligence can improve decision-making and perhaps even alter the competitive landscape. Highly recommended.

Bob Thompson, Founder and CEO, CustomerThink Corp. and author, *Hooked On Customers: The Five Habits of Legendary Customer-Centric Companies*

AI has the power to augment decision-making, but the challenge remains of how it deals with future unknown conditions. For example, if an algorithm only recognizes male or female genders, how do you ensure a transgendered person doesn't get labeled as either male or female? Until we have a way to account for unknown future conditions, we won't have a way to prevent unintended bias in our calculations.

Kristina Bergman, CEO and Founder, Integris Software Inc.

This book had me at "Stop making businesses more data focused; make data more business focused." Donal's incomparable view of how Data and AI should be serving me is inspiring. The machine is the assistant, not the overlord. **TOMORROW | TODAY** will be by my side moving forward.

Maureen Blandford, CMO, Software Improvement Group

TOMORROW TODAY

How AI Impacts How We Work, Live and Think
(and it's not what you expect)

Donal Daly

Published by OAK TREE PRESS
www.oaktreepress.com / www.SuccessStore.com

© 2016 Donal Daly

A catalogue record of this book is available from the British Library.

ISBN 978 1 78119 263 4 (Paperback)
ISBN 978 1 78119 264 1 (ePub)
ISBN 978 1 78119 265 8 (Kindle)
ISBN 978 1 78119 266 5 (PDF)
ISBN 978 1 78119 267 2 (Hardback)

CONTENTS

FOREWORD

INTRODUCTION   1

SECTION 1: HUMANS IN THE CENTER

1: WILL ARTIFICIAL INTELLIGENCE REPLACE KNOWLEDGE WORKERS?   24

2: AUGMENTED INTELLIGENCE MAXIMIZES HUMAN POTENTIAL   41

3: THE AUGMENTED JOURNEY   54

4: AUGMENTED INTELLIGENCE FOR KNOWLEDGE WORKERS   70

5: THE BIG DATA CONUNDRUM   90

6: AUGMENTED ANALYTICS   104

7: WHERE TO NEXT?   119

SECTION 2: INSIDE THE MACHINE

8: AN INTRODUCTION TO MACHINE LEARNING   130

9: ALGORITHMIC BIAS—KEEPING HUMANS IN THE LOOP   145

INDEX   161

FIGURES

1   WHAT HAPPENED IN AN INTERNET   2
    MINUTE (AUGUST 1, 2016)

2   THE FIVE MOST VALUABLE COMPANIES IN   7
    THE WORLD (AUGUST 1, 2016)

3   20M+ USERS TAKE TO THE STREET,   12
    PLAYING POKÉMON GO (JULY 2016)

4   FAVORITE LINKEDIN FUNCTIONS   13

5   THE KNOWLEDGE CURVE   25

6   THE IMPACT OF ROBOTS AND   39
    COMPUTERS ON WORK DONE BY
    HUMANS

7   KASPAROV'S CHESS TOURNAMENT   44
    RESULTS

8   YOUNG CHILDREN AND OLDER PEOPLE   50
    AS A PERCENTAGE OF GLOBAL
    POPULATION: 1950–2050

9   DMV REPORT OF A TRAFFIC ACCIDENT   55
    INVOLVING AN AUTONOMOUS VEHICLE

10 THE EASY-MILE SELF-DRIVING VEHICLE   57

11 NHTSA's LEVELS OF AUTONOMY FOR   58
    SELF-DRIVING VEHICLES

12 GOOGLE MAPS: CORK TO WATERVILLE   67

13	SALESFORCE DAILY TRANSACTION VOLUME—TUESDAY IS ALMOST ALWAYS BUSIEST	74
14	SALESFORCE's AI-RELATED ACQUISITIONS	77
15	MOBILE MAX	82
16	MAX INSIGHT EDITOR—RULES, ADVICE AND CONTEXT EDITED IN A SIMPLE GUI	85
16	MAX IN A SALESFORCE OPPORTUNITY RECORD	87
18	ALTIFY MAX: AUGMENTED INTELLIGENCE INSIGHT ENGINE	88
19	WORLDWIDE ENTERPRISE SOFTWARE REVENUE BY SUBSEGMENT 2010–2017 (US$ million)	98
20	HINDSIGHT, INSIGHT AND FORESIGHT	105
21	DATA AND THE FOUR STAGES OF ANALYTICS	111
22	AND GOD SAID ...	115
23	SIRI RESPONSES—1	124
24	SIRI RESPONSES—2	124
25	PREVIOUS HITS AND THEIR CHART POSITIONS	134
26	AN ALGORITHM TO PREDICT HIT SONGS	134
27	APPLYING THE ALGORITHM	135
28	WEIGHTING THE ELEMENTS OF THE ALGORITHM	136
29	APPLYING THE EXTENDED ALGORITHM	136
30	GOOGLE SEARCH RESULTS FOR "HOW OLD IS STEPHEN TYLER?"	138
31	FACEBOOK PHOTO TAGGING	140

32	GOOGLE SEARCH RESULTS: PAID AND ORGANIC	149
33	GOOGLE SEARCH RESULTS FOR "WOMEN SHOULDN'T HAVE"	150
34	GOOGLE SEARCH RESULTS FOR "MEN SHOULDN'T HAVE"	151
35	PROPUBLICA RECIDIVISM EXAMPLES	154
36	HUMAN-IN-THE-LOOP SYSTEM	156
37	SOCIETY-IN-THE-LOOP SYSTEM	157

TABLES

1 BIG DATA FORECASTS 2014–2026 (US$ 96
   billion)

2 FORECAST CAGR   96

3 BIG DATA FORECASTS 2014–2026 (US$ 97
   billion) WITH CAGR

DEDICATION

To those, like my late father, who work hard to get ahead, to go higher, but never look down on those below them.

FOREWORD

It wasn't that long ago I was walking towards a trade show at the Mandalay Bay in Las Vegas, and noticed this image—and while I may have actually seen it dozens of time, this time it really spoke to me.

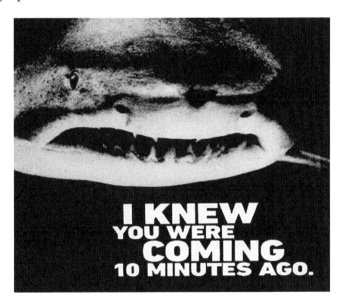

Although it was an advertisement for the "Shark Reef" exhibit, I was at a sales conference, and it got me thinking about this notion of a smarter more informed sales rep who can anticipate what customers will do next and change their behavior because of it.

Can digital marketing, social listening, personalized content and deeper customer segmentation provide the right insights to create the *'perfect quota killing sales machine'* (similar to this Great White)? Will marketing really be able to track a customer's journey and engage in meaningful ways to improve the customer experience? Will companies be able to 'smell the blood in the water' when a customer is ready to buy and make the transaction effortless? Will sales reps embrace all the insights marketing can provide to make them smarter sellers? Those seem to be the million dollar questions!

Is there a role for Artificial Intelligence? I will get to that in a minute and give you my personal opinion—

Let's for a moment make the assumption B2B companies are able to build these type of capabilities—the real question then becomes: "Will the sales organizations be agile and responsive (read fast) enough to change what they are doing in real time to become a *customer led sales organization*?" There is no question that the data can make reps smarter (if they can actually use it). But what data can't do is overcome the internal inertia that actually may be what is holding sales performance back. Sometimes the greatest inhibitor to transforming a sales organization is the sales leadership itself (yes, I know I actually said that out loud). The muscle memory and DNA of historically successful sales organizations can actually stand in the way of making the necessary changes. History is not always a predictor of the future, though we can certainly learn from it.

As Donal says in **TOMORROW | TODAY**, the problem is not that there is a deficit in information; the problem is that there is a deficit in insight. The reality is that the need to transform isn't about the sales team, or any customer-facing function, doing a bad job; *it is all about the customer.*

Unfortunately, *the unintended consequence of many technology advancements (social, mobile, cloud and information) is the power has shifted to the customer and towards the buyer's process;* and that changes everything.

Enterprise businesses, your customers, did not just magically get smarter. The confluence of cloud, mobile, and vast quantities of data, with the evolution of smart technologies like Artificial and Augmented Intelligence, Big Data and Machine Learning, has enabled them to evolve and adapt. For commercial organizations interacting with these enterprises, emulating that behavior is what will separate winners from losers.

The breakthrough occurs when we first accept that we need to change, that the landscape is different, and that we can choose whether this is an opportunity or a threat. The threat is real and you can decide whether to ignore it and suffer the consequences or turn that into an opportunity. In my 10 years at Gartner and in my current role at Salesforce I have seen many changes. My focus is on helping companies re-imagine how they can not only grow bigger but grow better with innovative business models and technology. I spend my time meeting with business leaders from some of the largest and most successful organizations in the world, to improve performance and enhance customer experience.

Today, we are at an inflection point for how businesses serve their customers. As it says in **Chapter 4**, we all "think for a living" and this is a time for reflection. AI, in its many forms, is shaping the future, and success will be impacted by how well we adopt that technology and adapt our practices to enable our companies to serve our customers.

For all the business leaders out there, it will be your job to convince your management that you need the freedom to take a few risks, explore the capabilities of AI within your sales, service and marketing efforts, and pilot new ways to organize how you enable your teams to consider new ways to engage. Otherwise a year from now we will all be having this same conversation (and you may be looking for a new job).

Tiffani Bova
Global, Customer Growth, Sales and Innovation Evangelist, Salesforce

INTRODUCTION

Sometimes out of the recesses of our minds a flicker of curiosity emerges. Is the pace of technological change a good thing? Sometimes it feels as if we are barely hanging on, buffeted by a constant torrent of innovation and evolution.

Do you sometimes wake up and wonder if today will be the day when, just for once, nothing changes? Imagine that one morning when you look at your email, your newsfeeds, or your social media accounts, nothing has happened, and there is no crisis to react to or fire to put out.

Perhaps that calm day might be tomorrow, or some day this week, but I really don't think so—not any time soon. The rapidity at which things happen in the world makes it hard to keep up.

On the Internet, the pace is staggering.

In one minute on August 1, 2016, the same day that technology took over the top five places in the stock market, this is what happened in an 'Internet minute' (see **Figure 1**).

Figure 1: WHAT HAPPENED IN AN INTERNET MINUTE
(AUGUST 1, 2016)

Activity	Per Internet Minute
Emails Sent	159,106,930
Google Searches	3,391,568
Blog Posts	3,154
Tweets	444,712
Videos viewed on YouTube	7,846,597
Photos uploaded to Instagram	44,814
Skype calls	135,946
Salesforce transactions	2,916,700
Internet Traffic (GB)	2,264,453
Emojis Sent	4,166,667

With so much activity it is impossible to keep up so we continue to filter our online experiences to experiences that we like, and to shut out counter-opinions or different perspectives. Driven by FOMO (fear of missing out) we're addicted to sending and receiving—there is little time for thought. And this starts at a very young age, with many kids getting their first smartphone by age 10. What they learn and how they experience the world at that formative age influences their values and subsequent behaviors.

Most of the developed world is drowning in data and inputs. Many people are addicted to notifications and updates—*homo interruptus* personified—powerless, and paralyzed, wondering if we should wait for the next trigger to proceed or if we have enough information to act now. This has become the victory of urgent over important.

One thing we know for sure: **we are all inundated with information**, but as Noam Chomsky, the American philosopher and cognitive scientist, said:

How is it that we have so much information, but know so little?

In 1934, T.S. Eliot, the poet and playwright wrote:

Where is the life we have lost in living?
Where is the wisdom we have lost in knowledge?
Where is the knowledge we have lost in information?

Eliot was in many ways presaging the Internet Age, the reality shared by Gen-Xers, Millennials and the upcoming Thumb Generation:[1] too much information—but too little insight. Millennials who are becoming an increasingly important force in the workplace are characterized by some as tech-savvy and proficient in applying technology to everyday problems efficiently.

But I wonder if the habits learned in an environment where the answer to everything is just a Google search away have in anyway reduced their critical faculties, removed the need to develop ideas from first principles, or through that journey to nourish their own perspective. If that is the case with Millennials and indeed with an increasingly large proportion of Gen-Xers—the term 'Millennials' is representative much more of a mindset than an age group—then we need to be careful that this trend does not continue with the Thumb Generation.

We want our future leaders to leverage the wisdom of others. As they do, they will see the horizon more clearly if they stand on the shoulders of those who have gone before them. We want them to respect the value of lessons learned

---

[1] **Thumb Generation:** This is a phrase that I came up with about two years ago watching my children and their friends exhibiting amazing dexterity with their thumbs as they texted and scrolled on their phones. I define this generation as those born between 1998 and 2010.

and to build on those lessons, and to stretch their minds, to extend those models, but we need them to seek insight, to learn the skills of primary research, to be inquisitive, curious and questioning, and above all to help create a better future, one that's founded in original thought. Ideas matter, and over the history of humans, ideas have continued to shape the world, and we need the best minds of the future to be well equipped to come up with fascinating and transformative ideas that will propel the species forward in a positive way.

This book is about the Insight Deficit,[2] and to an extent the Trust Quandary,[3] how to make sense of it all, and what you might do about it. It is about Artificial Intelligence (AI), but more importantly about *Augmented* Intelligence, a capability that enables us to create a present, a today, where we optimize human potential, understanding that tomorrow is already upon us. It explores Big Data and data science, Predictive, Prescriptive, and Descriptive Analytics, scrutinizing the hyperbolic claims of the most vocal proponents to uncover the real practical opportunities that Big Data provides to 'the rest of us,' not just the Big Five technology companies. It touches on the impact on our lives of social media, reflecting on the noise, the dilution in the value of connections, now that we all have so many, but highlighting the social, global and commercial benefits that this modern-day collaborative communication affords.

And then there is the *Internet*. Before the Internet we used to find jobs by reading through the Employment section of the local newspaper. Now we use LinkedIn and specialized job

---

[2]   **Insight Deficit**: A notion that because we have so much information we do not have the time to consider it and understand its meaning.

[3]   **Trust Quandary**: The decline in trust in government, authority and big machine, soon to extend to too much or too little trust in machines.

sites to match our career aspirations with global employers. Gone are the days of classified ads for *"SWF looking for partner with GSOH."* If you're a single white female seeking a partner with a good sense of humor, you're more likely to be one of the 66 million members of eHarmony, 438 of whom on average get married every day having found their soul mate online.[4]

Now, with the Internet of Things, it is not just people who are online. Signals from people and machines comingle to create a web of connections to control our lives:

- **GlowCaps** fit prescription bottles with a wireless chip that help people stick with their prescription regimen; from reminder messages, all the way to refill and doctor coordination.

- British drinks company **Diageo** has fitted 'smart' labels to its Johnnie Walker Blue Label whiskey to give the consumer an interactive experience, with messaging sent to the whiskey drinker's phone from the label.

- The **Mimo** infant monitor provides parents with real-time information about their baby's breathing, skin temperature, body position, and activity level on their smartphones.

- **Disney World** has created MagicBand, a wristband containing RFID tags, easing the journey through the amusement park for guests and allowing Disney to track visitors' movements through their properties.

- Smart thermostats like **Nest** use sensors, real-time weather forecasts, and the actual activity in your home

---

[4]   2009 survey conducted for eHarmony by Harris Interactive® online, see eHarmony.com.

during the day to reduce your monthly energy usage by up to 30%.

- **Fitness First** has invested in iBeacon technologies to track who exactly is entering their gyms and to send information to them automatically.

- Smart outlets like the **WeMo** allow you to instantly turn on and off any plugged-in device from across the world using your smartphone.

The world has donned an electronic skin and the Internet is the exoskeleton. The question is: *"Where is the heart?"* Tim O'Reilly, the person to whom many attribute the popularization of the terms *open source* and *Web 2.0*, prefers to modify the name *The Internet of Things* to *The Internet of Things and Humans*. The human factor and societal impact is explored extensively throughout the book.

Technology on Top

On August 1, 2016, for the first time ever, the five most valuable public companies in America were technology companies (see **Figure 2**), surely underlying how much impact the digital economy has on the world. These are the companies that are shaping the Internet and shaping our lives.

Figure 2: THE FIVE MOST VALUABLE COMPANIES IN THE WORLD (AUGUST 1, 2016)

Market Capitalization as of August 1, 2016 vs. Total Revenues 2015

Source: "The Five Most Valuable Companies in America All Have this in Common," Fortune, August 2016

As technology seeps further into the everyday domain of knowledge workers in business, there is both risk and opportunity.

Because we are constantly pounded by so much external stimulus we tend to filter the input, select our preferences and consume that which only confirms our own inherent biases. That is not a way to learn. It does not build a network of trust. It does nothing to increase our insight. It is not how we will experience different thinking and thereby broaden our own outlook.

Because we are under increasing pressure to act now and get results now, we can sometimes prioritize faster over better.

Because, as Moore's Law predicted, the computer processing power available to us now is almost limitless, and so we abrogate our responsibility to process input ourselves, and lose the habit of curiosity and self-determination.

Just because *"Customers who bought this also bought that,"* and I can *"Buy now with 1-Click®"* doesn't mean that I should do either. It means that I can, or I can decide to consider other options better suited to my needs, or I can choose to buy nothing at all.

The risk is that we don't stop and fully consider how to apply these technological advancements to our betterment. Most successful advances result from a conscious purposeful search for innovation opportunities. They are rarely accidental and they demand an uncommon level of domain-specific knowledge to be successful. Today's technology enables innovations in processes, products and marketplaces at a pace we have never seen before. In addition to the technological advances, successful innovation requires ingenuity, focus and, above all else, insight into the problem being solved. That demands deep domain knowledge— particularly when applied to knowledge workers.

The growth of data, data sources and the interconnectivity of all devices, simultaneously poses challenges and possibilities. Data volumes are exploding. More data has been created in the past two years than in the entire history of the human race. Data is growing faster than ever before and by the year 2020, our accumulated digital universe of data will have grown from 4.4 zeta bytes today to around 44 zeta bytes, or 44 trillion gigabytes. That's a 10-fold increase in just four years. But yet, while data scientists and the proponents of predictive analytics confer panacea-like properties on Big Data solutions, less than one-half of 1 percent of the world's data is even analyzed.

I wonder when we will realize that **there is no deficit in information; there is a deficit in insight**—and that insight is not solely the dominion of machines.

The Arrival of Artificial and Augmented Intelligence

The explosion of AI solutions proffers some hope. But it is worth questioning whether the rapidity of developments in AI will replace or augment the timeworn value of critical thinking. Maybe it will instead blunt the edge of inventiveness in the pursuit of automation rather than innovation or insight. As Nate Silver concluded in his seminal publication, *The Signal and the Noise*, the optimum solution is a combination of data, science and human judgment, the last based on knowledge and experience.

I began my AI journey when I started my first company in 1986. In 1988 I wrote a book called *Expert Systems Introduced*. Its purpose was to demystify, for the business person, much of the enigma that was AI at that time, shrouded, as it was, in academic publications replete with inaccessible language. My goal back then was to deliver AI or expert systems for the *rest of us*. In hindsight that aspiration was perhaps a little premature.

But now AI is exploding. With IBM's Watson, Apple's Siri, Microsoft's Cortana, Google's increasingly smart search engine, and Douglas Lenat's Cyc, this goal of AI in everyone's hand is perhaps now attainable. I am particularly excited about the work that Salesforce is doing in this area, democratizing AI in the same way that it has revolutionized cloud computing for all businesses.

In *Expert Systems Introduced* I described an expert system as follows:

> An expert system (AI) makes or saves money by codifying and encapsulating the knowledge of an expert in a system that makes it available to, and easily consumable by, a non-expert.

If I were to modify the definition today, I would make two changes:

> An expert system (AI) makes or saves money <u>or time</u> by codifying and encapsulating the knowledge of an expert in a system that makes it available to, easily consumable <u>and actionable</u> by a non-expert.

Time has become the most valuable currency for knowledge workers, and accordingly I have added *'or time'* to the definition. The addition of *'and actionable'* to the definition possibly panders somewhat to the increasing desire for *results now* rather than *thinking now and results later*, but is nonetheless valid. However, the most important aspect I want to highlight in the definition is one I have not changed in 30 years. **The encapsulation of knowledge is the foundation on which any true smart system is built.** Each of Watson, Google, Cyc, and the other examples mentioned above are built on its own bedrock of knowledge.

The Need for Thought

It is evident that the success of any knowledge-based business or human endeavor is dependent on the reasoning ability of the people involved. A growth mindset, curiosity, problem solving, deductive reasoning and an ability to cast aside the box, rather than just think outside it, are indicators of success.

I ask myself whether you can be an innovative leader in a specific knowledge domain if you can't absorb copious quantities of prior knowledge and then process laterally and intuitively to improve upon previous methods. What might happen in your own business if, every time you need to solve a particular problem, you and all your colleagues had the muscle memory of a million similar engagements from the past? Imagine if you had an always-accurate reflection of what worked well or where the objective was not achieved, and you knew the root cause of success or failure. Productivity would soar.

Now consider the more common situation—everyone starts from a blank slate each time. Clearly the former scenario is preferable. Embedded knowledge matters, whether it is in your mind or on your machine.

I was recently told a story about a young graduate who was interviewing for a position as a Business Analyst. Exploring the candidate's problem solving ability, one of the interviewers asked, *"How would you go about figuring out how many golf balls you could fit in an Airbus A380?"* Most of the other candidates talked about calculating the free space on the plane, and the most efficient way to pack golf balls into that space—but the graduate in the story took a different approach. She just pointed to her smartphone and said, *"Heck, I'd just Google it and get on to the next problem."*

Though many of us are seemingly now *just wired that way*, we need to remember that technology changes at a faster pace than people adapt, and sometimes, there are unintended consequences. (This is not a criticism of the Millennials who are much maligned, just a commentary on the mindset.)

Figure 3: 20M+ USERS TAKE TO THE STREETS, PLAYING POKÉMON GO (JULY 2016)

Will Augmented Reality change reality? As the 21 million phone clutching daily active Pokémon GO users hit the streets in July 2016 in search of Pokémon, health experts, social scientists, and developers alike have speculated as to its impact. I can't comment on the global impact, but I've see kids who would never get off a couch chasing through parks—but I wonder if they see the trees, or smell the grass. The phone has become the window on the world, and not just for Pokémon GO users.

When so many of us view the world through a four-inch rectangle of black glass—addicted as we are to our smartphones—is our peripheral vision impaired or our lateral thinking stunted? If you can't swipe, tap or pinch your way to your destination, will you give up on the endeavor because you have become accustomed to always-on, always-connected, instant gratification? Life was never that easy, nor does it need to be. It has much more texture than that.

The world has at once become available and accessible. However, it is in danger of becoming more shallow, more sound-bite, less considered, more homogenous, less diverse, and still less tolerant of diversity. Technology is a sometimes-unwitting accomplice in this malaise, thinning the fabric of human touch.

There is a reason why the most frequently visited page on LinkedIn is 'Who's Viewed Your Profile'. If more people viewed my profile than yours, does that mean I am more important than you? What's my score?

Figure 4: FAVORITE LINKEDIN FUNCTIONS

Users who find the function useful

Function	Percentage
Who's viewed your profile	75.7%
People you may know	63.3%
Direct messaging	50.2%
Searching for companies	45.3%
Advanced people searching	43.3%
Posting in group discussions	41.7%
Following companies	41.4%
Who's viewed your updates	39.8%
Posting status updates	38.9%
Reviewing "who knows whom"	36.9%
People also viewed	33.1%
Review of network updates (front page)	32%
Jobs function	28.9%
Searching for people in groups	26.4%

Source: Wayne Breitbarth via Forbes

Technology has created and eulogized the micro-moment and the gamified scorecard—promulgating multi-level achievements as the only end that matters. In this case, the endgame is the endgame—only results matter, and the once lustrous and enriching tapestry that is the journey is lost.

Sometimes it seems that everyone wants to be an icon; prestige and reputation is measured in followers and friends, views and likes. Is this iconic status a prerequisite to achievement or contribution, or a valid pursuit in its own right? I don't think so.

While opportunities abound, increased impatience and an orientation towards measurable and visible results can impair progress—though that may at first seem counterintuitive. The question we must ask ourselves is: *"How do all of these developments, these schizophrenic harbingers of both advancement and decline, shape how we think about the world, our place in it, and the impact we have?"*

Two Sides on Every Coin

Let me be clear. This is a time of great opportunity. Technology has enabled an unparalleled velocity of innovation, collaboration and communication. There has never been a time like this. Individuals can do more with their minds than ever before. Innovation exposes new ways to do the tasks that we struggle with today and exposes new possibilities that were heretofore impossible. How this plays out is yet to be determined, but the choices we make are important. The coin has been flipped towards the sky and, as it is spins in air, we get to influence how it lands.

This started as a business book, a sales book, or a guide for sellers, relationship builders and their leaders. It began as a reflection on Big Data and the danger of conclusions presented without any reflection, because we know that **there is too much *Big Data* and there are too few *big questions*.** I wanted to bring to life the possibilities of AI, but also to share a perspective that **AI should in fact stand for Augmented Intelligence**—blending the best of human and machine— rather than Artificial Intelligence. **Don't we all in fact think for a living?** I sought to explore the assumption that Millennials are all tech-savvy digital natives, but I now feel the need to juxtapose 'tech-dependent' alongside that.

Because technology has become an extension of the knowledge worker's business and personal life, it has become apparent that to separate the two is not just pointless, it is impossible.

This book has evolved to consider how technology impacts the human condition of knowledge workers as the fulcrum upon which we all teeter, in business and in life. How do we connect it all together, recognizing that the context for our derivations and deductions is frequently lacking and always changing? I am taking you on a journey, and hoping that in due course you too will arrive at a destination better able to answer some of these questions.

On the Shoulders of Giants

Steve Jobs proclaimed that you couldn't connect the dots into the future. In fact, he said:

> You can't connect the dots looking forward, you can
> only connect them looking backwards. So you have to trust
> that the dots will somehow connect in your future.

To trust that connection, you have to understand the forces that are at play. You have to first consider and understand the dots, before you can connect them. Do the work, expand your knowledge, deliberate on the details, then you can trust your informed instinct to connect the dots.

Albert Einstein defined insanity as doing the same thing over and over again and expecting different results. Does that imply (somewhat perversely) that, if you do the same things over and over again, you may in fact be able to connect dots into the future? That wasn't Dr. Einstein's point—but patterns that repeat can matter and inform but only when they point to informed causations, and not spurious correlations.

Pierre-Simon Laplace, the 19th century French mathematician, theorized that, given perfect knowledge, we could make perfect predictions. That we know is true, but the pursuit of perfect knowledge is endless; the pursuit of domain-specific knowledge less so.

Perhaps somewhere in the mélange of these three geniuses' perspectives is the truth. As we trend towards perfect knowledge, albeit in limited domains, we increase our ability to shape our future behavior through intelligently derived insights.

This time, this time today, right now, is a time to stop and think, to consider the dots, and to evaluate the patterns. **It is time to value and respect the need for knowledge and critical assessment, and then do something about it**. Reacting to time pressures, the need for immediate corporate results and personal gratification, rewarding ourselves, or being rewarded by others, getting the job done and moving on—we don't always take the time to deliberate. In corporate-land we juggle the fridge-magnet vocabulary of business-speak without critical assessment. We consume bumper sticker pronouncements in 140-character chunks without taking the time to digest. But we continue to ingest—and we are in danger of making ourselves sick.

But maybe all of this technology is actually making us more human again. Does the speed of interaction mean that we have to think more about who we are trying to reach or influence, how we connect, how they connect, how we share, how we discover? You have to feel it, let it touch you, and never forget that it touches others. Maybe that is a good thing.

And So Onwards

I have been privileged to learn from my interactions with great business leaders and visionaries in some of the most innovative companies in the world. What is written here has been shaped by these and many others: leading thinkers, artists, scientists, writers, musicians, innovators, and philanthropists. At times, their perspective has certainly challenged mine—and most of the time, they were right and I was wrong. But I have always been enriched by these encounters. I have endeavored to learn from their experiences and to borrow their wisdom.

Nothing will halt the advancement of software innovation, nor impede the progress in Artificial or Augmented Intelligence. This is a good thing. These developments present us with great opportunities. Behind every data point, social media trigger, and connected signal is a connected person or business, clicking a mouse or pinching a screen and looking to learn or progress. People are at the core and the data isn't accidental; there is just too much of it.

The insight breakthrough can happen when we first recognize that the value is not just in the data itself, the number of social connections or the technical capabilities alone. We have the opportunity and the obligation to guide the outcome. It's our place and our responsibility in the world. Utility, when coupled with intelligently directed application of that utility, is the path to insight. When we know the important questions to ask, and the critical problems that need to be solved, we have the signposts for a journey to insight—to a society that will be augmented by technology for sure, but a society in which we all want to participate. We should accept that there will be failed attempts—success is often preceded by failure—but when we take the time to infuse the technology with knowledge and experience, our path to increased insight will be more secure and we can reach a more informed destination more easily.

TOMORROW | TODAY navigates the impact of AI on business professionals in the knowledge economy—Sales, Marketing, and Customer Service—and it demystifies Artificial and Augmented Intelligence, Machine Learning and Big Data in that context. It will guide you to embrace the arrival of AI (particularly the Augmented variety) as a positive force for knowledge workers, placing humans at the center, supported by the machine. The book helps you decide what tasks, currently being undertaken by knowledge workers, can be offloaded to computers and how to augment your most value-add activities—for example, strategic sales, marketing strategy, and customer engagement—with Augmented Intelligence. Solving this problem will deliver rapid competitive advantage, today and tomorrow.

A Short Outline of the Book

This is not a book for technologists *per se*, but more a book about how technology impacts all of our businesses and all of our lives. It is written primarily for business leaders. Now, more than ever, this is a time when we should pause and think. Important and balanced decisions need to be made to maximize human potential, and those decisions should be based on insight, as much of it as we can harvest.

It is a book for all knowledge workers: in Sales, Marketing, Customer Service, and Product Management—the entire Revenue Team—but also for those in supporting back-office functions like HR, Operations and Finance, and Legal and Procurement, those often under-appreciated functions that keep the show on the road.

It is intended to provide a general understanding of the technological advancements that are impacting our world to equip business leaders with enough knowledge to consider the inevitable impact on business of these advancements. I hope too that it provides enough to prompt a considered perspective on technology's impact on our world, today and tomorrow.

Chapter 1 takes a brief tour through Artificial Intelligence, exploring the advancing role of machines as they move inexorably along the knowledge curve, heading up and to the right. Is AI an existential threat, as suggested by some commentators? How can we prepare for these changes? Is the future of knowledge workers secure or what changes will be needed? I take an example and look at the projected impact on sales professionals and wonder when the machine wins, and when instead the human remains at the center. Our jobs will inevitably change and we must prepare for that.

Chapter 2 examines Augmented Intelligence, the real hidden gem—in which lies the opportunity to maximize human potential. We can indeed put aside our concern about robot overlords and ask ourselves, *"What is the role of Augmented Intelligence in the workplace today?"* and *"What is it going to mean to sales professionals, enterprise marketing leaders or other knowledge workers?"* The short answer is that the future is bright. In fact, there has never been a better time to be a knowledge worker.

Chapters 3 and 4 take us through two separate journeys—technology and business—the first a blueprint or analog for the second. The evolution of the driverless car and mapping technologies like Google Maps touches so many parts of our lives. The story by itself is fascinating and filled with ingenuity and creativity. What is the equivalent in business? How can these enhancements propel knowledge workers forward, moving them up the knowledge curve faster than the machine? Sales professionals, consultants, marketers and others have an exciting future. Salesforce has made some very interesting moves in this area and in **Chapter 4** you will also see a practical example of Augmented Intelligence for the sales function from a Salesforce partner.

In **Chapters 5 and 6,** Big Data and Analytics, the other side of the AI coin, are explored. First by describing the role of Big Data in AI, and peeling back the layers on this very topical subject, the book answers the questions that you might be asking yourself: *"Do I need Big Data or just Analytics?"* and *"What's the difference?"* The four different types of analytics are explained, along with the role of humans in each one. Common pitfalls are highlighted and suggested approaches to avoid them explained. Analytics may be the pathfinder, but the human still needs to hold the compass.

Chapter 7 is called 'Where To Next?' and here we look at what we have learned so far, and take a peek into the future of what AI means today, to see what it will mean to the future of knowledge workers and what you should do about it.

You could stop here; but in a separate section, **Inside the Machine**, there are two final chapters that provide greater insight into what is going on in the guts of the computers and minds of the engineers and programmers who designed them.

Chapter 8 provides a high-level overview of Machine Learning (ML), demonstrating the need for very large datasets to exist before this technology can be effective. With some examples from Google, you will see how your input to the machine is making the machine smarter, and you will learn if ML is a threat or opportunity for you as an individual, and how it might change the world in which your business operates.

Chapter 9: There is a natural human tendency to be biased, and the inevitable consequence is that, as we program algorithms into machines, these machines will also exhibit bias. We should be aware of this and consider whether there is a need for a national or global forum to mitigate any negative impact as we recognize that there is also tremendous upside potential and opportunity.

Finally, I'm very hopeful for the world in which we live. I am optimistic about the future of knowledge workers. But I know that you have to make decisions every day to prepare for that future. This book is intended to be your companion on that journey, equipping you to pause for thought, and to consider the important questions first, lest you stumble towards accidental answers.

This book is about **TOMORROW | TODAY: HOW AI IMPACTS HOW WE WORK, LIVE, AND THINK (AND IT'S NOT WHAT YOU EXPECT).**

HUMANS IN THE CENTER

CHAPTER 1

WILL ARTIFICIAL INTELLIGENCE REPLACE KNOWLEDGE WORKERS?

If I remove 'knowledge' from this chapter title and extend AI to include automation, it is very easy to answer the question in the affirmative. There is definitely a cadre of workers who have already been replaced by technology—for example:

- Who calls directory information anymore to get a phone number?
- You don't call a travel agent to reserve a hotel room or check available flights.
- Booking a taxi is no longer the exclusive preserve of the taxi dispatcher.
- Securing a table at the restaurant is just a few taps on your phone.
- Buying online is the quickest growing retail channel and most of that workflow is automated.

The humans who were the providers of these services have been displaced.

But as we move up the knowledge curve the answer becomes less clear. Can computers reason in more complex domains and replace knowledge workers that need to apply judgment?

Figure 5: THE KNOWLEDGE CURVE

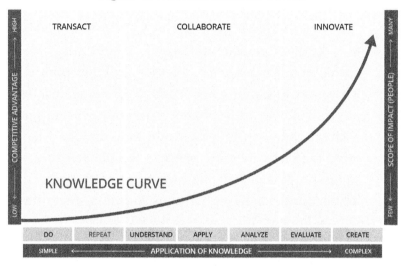

This is not a new idea. Since the early 1900s futurists, science fiction writers and scientists have grappled with and debated the notion of computers as sentient beings that could emulate or exceed the thinking capacity of humans:

- As early as 1939, in his Robot short stories, science fiction writer Isaac Asimov equipped his robots with the *positronic* brain that simulated a consciousness comparable to the human form. Even then, the notion of protecting humans from rogue robots was addressed. Asimov's *The Three Laws of Robotics* stipulated that robots could not injure humans, robots would obey humans and robots would not self-injure.

- The Turing test, developed by Alan Turing in 1950, tested a machine's ability to exhibit intelligent behavior equivalent to, or indistinguishable from, that of a human. Turing introduced the test in his paper, *Computing Machinery and Intelligence*, while working at the University of Manchester. It opens with the words: *"I propose to consider the question, 'Can machines think?'"*

- In 1980, the American philosopher John Searle, currently in residence as professor of philosophy as University of California, Berkeley, argued against the position that an appropriately programmed computer with the right inputs and outputs would thereby have a mind in exactly the same sense as human beings— suggesting that a program cannot give a computer a 'mind,' 'understanding' or 'consciousness,' regardless of how intelligently it may make it behave.

Even though these debates have raged for the best part of a century, the AI arguments have become polemic in recent times. There is a growing fear of the negative consequences of smart machines. This concern is sometimes uninformed, often reasoned, and other times fueled by denial or emotion. We can debate whether the fear is based on an emotional reaction to a perceived power-shift to the machine, whether it is rational and established on a considered foundation of research and knowledge, or an illogical position or unsound reasoning. In any case the anxiety typically stems either from the predictions of commentators who forecast a future where all or most workers will be replaced by robots, or in the case where super-intelligence is present, apprehension as a result of the apocalyptic scenarios depicted in movies where the real-world future assumes *Skynet-like* characteristics. (You might recall from the *Terminator* movie franchise that Skynet is a <u>fictional</u> conscious, artificial general intelligence system that gained self-awareness after it had spread into millions of computer servers all across the world and then sought to exterminate the human race. Realizing the extent of its abilities, its creators tried to deactivate it.)

If you conduct a Google search on *"Can robots replace"* you will find nearly 10 million search results. Various contributors suggest that job functions, including doctors, lawyers, accountants, office clerks, pharmacists, and babysitters, can be replaced by machines. Even back in 2012, highly respected Internet guru Vinod Khosla predicted that the future of medical practice would be more robot than doctor. Algorithms operated by devices seeded with Artificial Intelligence would provide objective analyses, he said, ones that physicians today largely cannot do because of embedded procedures and hackneyed ways of thinking about healthcare. This led Khosla to conclude that at least 80 percent of doctors could be replaced by software.

The question that I want you to consider is what the positive or negative impact will be on knowledge workers in business. We need to consider the consequences for those in Sales, Marketing, Customer Service, and Product Management—the customer-facing functions—and also think about the repercussions for those in the back-office. If we learn anything from history, we know that each technological paradigm shift in the past has catapulted the entire human workforce forward.

In this instance we may need to reflect on how to best leverage the advancements but be prepared to respond to the negative impacts that may set certain segments back. In 2015 the World Economic Forum (WEF) predicted a 'Fourth

Industrial Revolution,' characterized by major advancements in Artificial Intelligence, robotics, and other technologies. According to the WEF, "… *current trends could lead to a net employment impact of millions of jobs lost to disruptive labor market changes over the period 2015–2020."* The WEF estimates that a grand total of 7.1 million jobs will be lost as a direct result of innovations, and that two-thirds of these jobs will be *"concentrated in the Office and Administrative job family."* Furthermore, some industries where machines already play a large part, like manufacturing and production, will see further robot substitution. On the upside, the WEF estimates that there will be an increase of 2 million jobs added as a consequence of innovation. The net loss of 5 million jobs may well be overstated, as the Forum also notes that humans *"retain relatively good potential for up-skilling, redeployment, and productivity enhancement through technology rather than pure substitution."*

This is the crucial point that I want to explore. Up-skilling will be crucial for humans looking to retain or attain employment, but rather than looking at this as an 'us *versus* them' scenario, the optimum result will be achieved when we combine what machines are good at with what humans are good at. I discuss this in detail in **Chapter 2**.

AI already has made a major impact on our lives and this impact curve is exponentially growing. As with any innovation in technology, from something as historically transformative as nuclear energy to the global pervasiveness of the Internet, there is the potential for both good and bad outcomes.

Nuclear energy is clean, efficient and cheap and today one in five US households and businesses is powered by nuclear energy. On the other hand, Chernobyl, Fukushima and Three

Mile Island are examples of extremely bad outcomes and, of course, the threat of nuclear weapons still looms large.

You probably wonder how we ever survived without the Internet. It is such a wonderful platform for information dissemination and personal and business collaboration. There is a lot that is positive, but there is a darker side and there are threats to contend with also. We have seen the near death of the music industry through online music theft. A 2014 report from McAfee suggests that the global cost of cyber-crime is more than $400 billion. And 86% of sex crimes with minors are now initiated from social sites. It's clear that, as with any major innovation, there are possibilities for both positive and negative results.

Some Concerns About AI

The rapid growth in advancements in AI makes it potentially one of the most significant developments of our time and it too will undoubtedly have both good and bad outcomes. In recent times some of the world's most prominent thinkers have expressed their concerns about the potential long-term threat of Artificial Intelligence:

> Success in creating AI would be the biggest event in human history. Unfortunately, it might also be the last, unless we learn how to avoid the risks. In the near term, world militaries are considering autonomous-weapon systems that can choose and eliminate targets. – **Stephen Hawking**

> I think we should be very careful about artificial intelligence. If I had to guess at what our biggest existential threat is, it's probably that. So we need to be very careful. I'm increasingly inclined to think that there should be some

> regulatory oversight, maybe at the national and
> international level, just to make sure that we don't do
> something very foolish. – **Elon Musk**

Bill Gates added some context:

> I am in the camp that is concerned about super
> intelligence. First the machines will do a lot of jobs for us
> and not be super-intelligent. That should be positive if we
> manage it well. A few decades after that though the
> intelligence will be strong enough to be a concern.

Because this is a complex area it can be hard to distinguish between what is called *weak AI* or *narrow AI*—a non-sentient computer intelligence or AI that is focused on one narrow task—and *strong AI* or *Artificial General Intelligence (AGI)*—a machine with consciousness, sentience and mind, with the ability to apply intelligence to any problem, rather than just one specific problem.

In today's world, all real-world systems labeled 'Artificial Intelligence' of any sort are weak AI at most, but are becoming more prevalent. Applications like Siri, Google Search, Nest, spelling and grammar checkers, Google Maps and self-parking cars are all examples of weak AI. Just because it is weak doesn't mean that it doesn't deliver value. These weak AI applications are giving us back time, removing friction in small leaps, not large ones, but ubiquitous leaps in almost every context.

I travel to San Francisco about once a month. When I land I open Uber on my smartphone and request a car. Because Uber knows where I am it knows what drivers nearby to notify. It knows how many cars are available and how long it will take for the driver to arrive. I am a creature of habit and Uber knows that. Most of the time when I land in San

Francisco I travel to the same hotel. Uber suggests the hotel destination. When I leave the hotel the following morning, the top suggested destination on Uber is my company's office on San Francisco's Sansome Street. Uber has learned about my habits. It is getting to know me and every time I take a ride it gets to know more. Of course, when I leave my office at the end of the week, Uber suggests that I want to go to San Francisco airport, and most of the time it is right. My trips to San Francisco have a little less friction and I didn't even notice it happening.

Each one of us that carries a smartphone gains benefit from business and personal productivity applications that use weak AI to deliver tremendous advantage. Design is at the heart of these weak AI applications, providing for a better user experience designed in from the start with emphasis on utility and relevance informed by AI. Mobile was the inflection point that enabled this paradigm shift and the phone has become the contextual hub for productivity. The AI is invisible and generally not apparent to us. Instead of teaching humans about computers we now subconsciously teach the machine about *us*. Most users don't understand how most AI applications work and we shouldn't need to. The key factor in these systems, however, is that **all AI needs to be taught**. The machines don't just wake up some day and figure out how to provide smart answers or intelligent responses to your questions. Someone had to infuse the software program with the knowledge in the first place.

When you call a customer service agent at your friendly bank and have a 'conversation' with an automated voice you are probably talking to an AI-powered device—just one that can be very frustrating at times. When you finally get to the

"Press 4 to speak to an agent," you have been guided through a decision tree that someone has designed.

Our world today is heavily populated with weak AI programs, where technology is applied to replace human tasks. These programs are far from sentient and are not the emotional or angry AI examples we see in science fiction. Nonetheless, they are very useful and will continue to become more useful and even more pervasive. The challenge that we face in business is to figure out the core AI elements that we can practically and pragmatically use today and how we augment their power with human intervention. We need to pay urgent attention to the application of AI for knowledge workers in business.

The Future for Knowledge Workers Is (Probably) Secure for Now

Think about these jobs for a second: user experience designer, data scientist, online community manager, cyber security specialist, augmented reality developer, SEO specialist, social media strategist, and 3D printing technologist. These jobs did not exist when our parents or grandparents were in the workplace. These new roles have been created to address new problems or opportunities that exist today because of the advancement of technology, and, at least in some part, offset the jobs that are being lost when human labor is replaced by technology.

Predicting that millions of jobs will be lost can make for great click-bait headlines. The truth, however, is not that simple or as stark. There is no question that, for certain workers, if they continue to perform the same tasks in the same way as before, ignoring the possibilities for change and improvement afforded by developments in technology, they are much more likely to face job extinction than if they adapt their work practices to leverage the advantages that technology provides.

"It is not the strongest / fittest of the species that survives, nor the most intelligent... It is the one that is the most adaptable to change" is usually attributed to Charles Darwin but was actually coined by Leon C. Megginson, Professor of Management and Marketing at Louisiana State University, who offered it as a paraphrase of Darwin's thinking first in a paper published in 1963. It captures the essence of the challenge that recent developments in AI present for knowledge workers.

First they need to determine how to leverage these innovations to find new approaches to execute the tasks they do today, and then to figure out how new tasks, previously considered difficult or impossible can be tackled.

The Business-to-Business or B2B salesperson is a great example of a knowledge worker who, if you believe the headlines, is at risk of extinction. In a report published in April 2015, Forrester Research forecasted that, out of a total of 4.5 million US B2B salespeople, one million would lose their jobs to technology by 2020. The argument is predicated on the premise that, while B2B buyers overwhelmingly prefer to research, and increasingly buy, products and services *via* a self-service website, B2B sellers still force buyers to interact with their salespeople as part of the purchase process. Forrester points out that B2B buyers are living in a digital-first world, and that B2B sellers must adapt.

While the headline of the Forrester report—*The Death of the B2B Salesman*—is a little over the top, the essence of the message, or, at least part of it, is valuable. If the B2B sellers, who are most at risk to being replaced by the Internet and self-service technology, do not adapt they will be replaced by technology.

Forrester identifies four main seller archetypes, listed here in order of 'likely to become extinct':

- **Order Takers:** Salespeople who work with a non-complex buyer dynamic and non-complex product or service.

- **Explainers:** Salespeople who work with a non-complex buyer dynamic and complex product or service.

- **Navigators:** Salespeople who work with a complex buyer dynamic and non-complex product or service.

- **Consultants:** Salespeople who work with a complex buyer dynamic and complex product or service.

Of these personas, Order Takers are projected to be most at risk. As Andy Hoar, principal analyst at Forrester, said at the 2015 Forrester Sales Enablement Forum, *"So as technology gets better at explaining things, we don't need humans to explain anymore."* At the other end of the spectrum, the Consultant category was viewed by Forrester as a growth category. *"Consultants are a qualitatively different bunch of people,"* Hoar said. *"They can explain abstract concepts; they can solution sell; they can build relationships. They're true consultants."*

The challenge for the leadership of these selling organizations is pretty clear. They need to figure out how to use innovation to up-skill those most at risk to areas where there is less exposure. Be mindful as well of the ripple effect on the knowledge workers who are not yet at risk... the up-skilled knowledge workers will potentially threaten the next level of knowledge worker if they too don't embrace the need to continually self-educate and up-skill. AI, particularly the Augmented Intelligence variant, provides great scope for these leaders to augment the skills of their employees to equip them to perform at higher levels.

When Does the Machine Win?

There are many things that machines are better suited to than humans. Machines don't get tired or emotional, are not subjective or judgmental in their assessment; they don't spend a lot of time in meetings, on social media sites, or reading emails; they don't get bored with repeating the same task—in fact, they seem to enjoy it; they rarely get interrupted by their family or in-laws, need to take vacation, or leave a task unfinished. If you need the same thing done over and over again, without variation, consistently, following a prescribed set of instructions, then the machine is your man (or woman) for the job.

On the other hand, machines are not good yet at nuance, judgment, reading body language, imagining different scenarios, solving problems that they have not been programmed to solve, managing people, dealing with sudden change, applying expertise without guidance, undertaking unpredictable physical tasks, interpreting patterns they have not been taught to recognize, or interacting with people. In fact, without explicit programming, there's a lot that machines are not good at, and these are mostly things at which humans are pretty adept.

The logical way forward is to combine the strengths of machines and humans to let the machines do what they are best suited to, and to free up time to allow humans to do what machines can't do. The mistake, however, would be to assume that, just because a computer is not doing your job today, it cannot do some part of it now, and maybe all of it in the future. Now is the time to consider how you can maintain your competitive value advantage over the computer by using the innovations that are available today to augment the value that you add.

Smart technologies such as Machine Learning and AI will represent an increasingly greater role in your personal life and their impact in the workplace will be significant. The question is not just whether AI will eliminate your job, but to what extent a job will be impacted. It will be transformative in your lifetime. The key is how to uncover the possibilities for innovative approaches to today's tasks and to learn enough about what is possible with narrow AI capabilities to perform new tasks that you may not have considered possible before.

In a July 2016 report, *Where Machines Could Replace Humans—and Where They Can't (Yet)*, from McKinsey & Company, the management consultancy firm, the authors suggest that there is nuance in the answer to the question in the report title:

> While automation will eliminate very few occupations entirely in the next decade, it will affect portions of almost all jobs to a greater or lesser degree, depending on the type of work they entail. – **McKinsey Quarterly, July 2016**

McKinsey points out that analyzing work activities rather than occupations is the most accurate way to examine the technical feasibility of automation. However, technical feasibility is a crude measure unless the task that is normally conducted by the human can be fully described in binary logical terms, and the domain expertise or knowledge that is applied by the knowledge worker 'without thinking' can be fully and completely infused into the software that is powering the automation.

McKinsey acknowledges that the hardest roles to automate with the technology available today are those that involve managing or developing people, or applying expertise to decision-making, planning or creative work. Tasks like coding software, managing a sales team, writing promotional materials, designing a product, or planning an engagement with a customer are all knowledge worker activities. Even when computers are used to crunch data, produce sales forecasts, or optimize trucking routes, humans are still necessary to understand what data matters, to interpret the results of the sales forecast, or embed experience and expertise into designing the optimum truck routes.

But It Will Not Affect Me—Yes, It Will

I have spoken at length to many professionals about the potential threat and opportunities from AI. Two things that are seemingly contradictory have struck me. Most of the people I spoke to recognize that automation in general, and AI in particular, will replace some of the work being done by knowledge workers today—although opinions vary as to how much of the work will be affected and how soon it will happen. However, most people do not expect their own roles to be materially influenced. This does not make sense.

Even for higher-end job functions a lot of time is spent collecting and processing data. According to McKinsey these activities have a potential for automation exceeding 60 percent and people whose annual incomes exceed $200,000 spend more than 30 percent of their time doing these tasks.

A March 2016 study from Pew Research, *Public Predictions for the Future of Workforce Automation*, underlines this perspective. According to Pew:

> A majority of Americans predict that within 50 years, robots and computers will do much of the work currently done by humans—but few workers expect their own jobs or professions to experience substantial impacts.

Further detail from the study suggests that 65% of Americans expect that robots or computers will do much of the work currently done by humans, but 80% expect that their own jobs or professions will remain largely unchanged and will exist in the current forms 50 years from now!

Figure 6: THE IMPACT OF ROBOTS AND COMPUTERS ON WORK DONE BY HUMANS

Two-thirds of Americans expect that robots and computers will do much of the work currently done by humans within 50 years...

% of adults who say that in the next 50 years robots and computers will do much of the work currently done by humans

...but most workers expect that their own jobs will exist in their current forms in five decades

% of workers who say the jobs / professions they work in now will / will not exist in 50 years

Note: Second chart based on those who are currently employed on a full- or part-time basis
Source: Survey conducted June 10 - July 12, 2015
PEW RESEARCH CENTER

How anyone could suggest that his or her job will not change in the next 50 years is staggering to me. You only have to look at what you can do on a smartphone today to see that nothing ever stays the same, and that the rate of technological progress is accelerating—for good, or bad.

Artificial Intelligence, Augmented Intelligence, Machine Learning, and Intelligent Algorithms are all being used widely today. In many cases the more obvious examples are consumer, not business, applications—but you only have to look at the developments of the consumer web as a foreteller of the business web to see that consumer behavior always predicts business behavior.

Although all consumers are not business people, all business people are consumers, and what we experience in consumer-land informs our expectation in business-land.

The advancements in technology—from self-driving vehicles and voice recognition systems, semi-autonomous robots to intelligent algorithms and Predictive Analytics tools—demonstrate that machines are increasingly capable of performing a wide range of jobs that have long been the preserve of humans.

If you care about the future of knowledge work and your place in it, it is probably time to understand how to apply these technologies to (part of) your job or your business. This is the essence of the promise of Augmented Intelligence, which I will explore in detail in **Chapter 2**.

AUGMENTED INTELLIGENCE MAXIMIZES HUMAN POTENTIAL

The opportunity for Augmented Intelligence is to maximize human potential—today.

We can put aside our concerns about robot overlords. The reality is that we have no idea yet how to explain human consciousness and we even struggle to define intelligence. We don't know what to build, much less how to build it. The latest estimates are that the human brain contains about 30 billion neurons in the cerebral cortex — the part of the brain associated with consciousness and intelligence. The 30 billion neurons of the cerebral cortex contain about 1,000 trillion synapses (connections between neurons). Without a detailed model of how synapses work on a neurochemical level, there's no hope of modeling how the brain works. Until we figure that out, the likelihood that we will see sentient computers is infinitesimally small. Certainly, this will not happen in the next three or four decades.

Those who argue that Moore's Law—the observation made in 1965 by Gordon Moore, co-founder of Intel, that the number of transistors per square inch on integrated circuits doubles every two years, and consequently the power of computer hardware grows exponentially—would deliver self-aware computers through computing power alone, are naïve and ignore the software limitations, best described by Wirth's Law. In 1995 Nicholas Wirth pointed out that software is getting slower more rapidly than hardware is getting faster. Even if that wasn't true, brute hardware power doesn't solve the problem.

According to Moore's Law, your PC should be 65,000 times more powerful than it was 25 years ago. Whether the math works out exactly, certainly personal computing devices today, including our smartphones and tablets, are dramatically  more powerful than the first IBM PC that was launched in August 1981.

The problem, though, is the software. Let's face it, your word processor just hasn't improved that much. It's certainly prettier, and it has some pretty cool functionality like spell checking and document publishing capabilities. But has it improved by even one order of magnitude, let alone five orders of magnitude? I don't think so.

The challenge is with the pace of change in software. Microsoft Windows is said to be the largest software product ever written at about 40 million lines of code—and like all software, there are a few bugs in there. The computer scientist

Peter Kassan estimates that a computer program that would simulate the cerebral cortex would be about 25 times more complex than Windows and would contain about 20 trillion errors that would have to be debugged. Even those who put forward computationalism—the notion that we can achieve general AI without having to simulate the brain—stumble when faced with the complexity of language and the world that we naturally assimilate every day.

Does this mean that all of the advancements in AI are without value, or that they will not have an impact on our society? Not at all; but it is the blend of human and machine intelligence that will prove to be more effective over the coming decades.

After his defeat by Deep Blue, IBM's chess-playing machine, Gary Kasparov, the world's greatest chess grandmaster, began exploring the interplay between man and computer and how each could affect the outcome of a game. Kasparov designed a tournament to determine which grouping would garner superior results—solely humans, solely computers, or a combination of humans and computers. Hundreds of matches were played.

As the tournament progressed it looked like the human experts had the upper hand. Three grandmasters, working very efficiently with support from computers and human colleagues, had eliminated almost all opponents. There was one exception—a team called ZackS, which had made it all the way from the qualifiers (required for non-titled players) all the way to the finals. As the tournament was being played on the Internet, no one knew who they were—just that there were no grandmasters among them.

Figure 7: KASPAROV'S CHESS TOURNAMENT'S RESULTS

The result of the final was a real shocker: ZackS defeated Russian grandmaster Vladimir Dobrov convincingly. But who was ZackS? It turned out that they were two amateur chess players from New Hampshire: Steven Cramton and Zackary Stephen, who used three personal computers to assist them in the event. No grandmasters or intelligent machines were involved.

The outcome astonished everyone. The formula for success was humans, augmented by machines.

"The surprise came at the conclusion of the event," Kasparov stated. *"The winner was revealed to be not a grandmaster with a state-of-the-art computer, but a pair of amateur American chess players using three computers at the same time."*

This serves as a great example of how combining the speed and processing power of a computer with a human's interpretive capabilities leads to superior results. And this is Augmented Intelligence in its basic form — computational algorithms helping to put the human end user in the best position to make an informed decision.

It may well be that some aspects of human thinking are machine-like, but human intelligence doesn't proceed in the methodical, brute force way that a computer works through problems. There is a limit to which human reasoning can really be boiled down to explicit algorithms. As yet, critical powers of human thought such as intuition, interpretation of context, or tolerance of ambiguity cannot be represented in an algorithmic way. Human and machine intelligence each bring something to the table. We should be careful to focus our efforts on those parts of the human thinking or reasoning process we can model for computers—lest we start modeling the human mind on computers.

There are already many tasks that computers have in hand, and it is wishful thinking to believe that human intelligence will add value in every application into the future. The ability to work well alongside machines will be increasingly essential. The way we are going to continue to progress is through human creativity applied in a humanistic / non-robotic way and augmented by the limited, but increasing, intelligence in machines. The purpose of Augmented Intelligence is to maximize human potential.

We Need Augmented Intelligence Today

Throughout this century, there have been warnings that technology would wipe out large numbers of middle class jobs. In the midst of the Great Depression, the economist John Maynard Keynes forecast that technological progress might allow a 15-hour workweek, and abundant leisure, by 2030. But around the same time, President Herbert Hoover received a letter warning that industrial technology was a "Frankenstein monster" that threatened to upend manufacturing, "devouring our civilization." (The letter came from the mayor of Palo Alto, of all places.) In 1962, perhaps more prescient than some of his contemporaries, President John F. Kennedy said, *"If men have the talent to invent new machines that put men out of work, they have the talent to put those men back to work."*

In 1961 a *TIME* magazine story expressed concern about *The Automation Jobless*:

> The number of jobs lost to more efficient machines is only part of the problem. What worries many job experts more is that automation may prevent the economy from creating enough new jobs ... Throughout industry, the trend has been towards bigger production with a smaller work force ... Many of the losses in factory jobs have been countered by an increase in the service industries or in office jobs. But automation is beginning to move in and eliminate office jobs too ... In the past, new industries hired far more people than those they put out of business. But this is not true of many of today's new industries ... Today's new industries have comparatively few jobs for the unskilled or semiskilled, just the class of workers whose jobs are being eliminated by automation.

Such concerns have recently regained prominence. In their book, *The Second Machine Age*, MIT scholars Erik Brynjolfsson and Andrew McAfee offer an unsettling picture of the likely effects of automation on employment:

> Rapid and accelerating digitization is likely to bring economic rather than environmental disruption, stemming from the fact that as computers get more powerful, companies have less need for some kinds of workers. Technological progress is going to leave behind some people, perhaps even a lot of people, as it races ahead. **As**

we'll demonstrate, there's never been a better time to be a worker with special skills or the right education, because these people can use technology to create and capture value. However, there's never been a worse time to be a worker with only 'ordinary' skills and abilities to offer, because computers, robots, and other digital technologies are acquiring these skills and abilities at an extraordinary rate.

Clearly, the progress in automation and technology over the last century has not made human workers obsolete. In fact, the quality of work has improved for most. As David Autor points out in his article, *Why Are There Still So Many Jobs? The History and Future of Workplace Automation*:

Tasks that cannot be substituted by automation are generally complemented by it... improvements in one do not obviate the need for the other.

I'm not blind to the threat on low-skilled jobs of automation. It is clear to me that AI is moving up the knowledge curve to address job functions, or parts thereof, of knowledge workers. But there are constraints on how far up the curve technology can go and, as Brynjolfsson and McAfee said *in The Second Machine Age*, **there's never been a better time to be a [knowledge] worker.** The scope of occupations that automation can effectively address is bounded because there are many tasks that people understand inherently but are hard to represent in binary structures. Autor refers to this constraint as Polanyi's Paradox, named after the economist, philosopher, and chemist who observed in 1966, *"We know more than we can tell."* Autor goes on to say:

When we break an egg over the edge of a mixing bowl, identify a distinct species of birds based on a fleeting

> glimpse, write a persuasive paragraph, or develop a
> hypothesis to explain a poorly understood phenomenon,
> we are engaging in tasks that we only tacitly understand
> how to perform. Following Polanyi's observation, the tasks
> that have proved most vexing to automate are those
> demanding flexibility, judgment, and commonsense—skills
> that we understand only tacitly.

Machine Learning is making some headway in overcoming Polanyi's Paradox. Give a machine enough training data about a not-too-complex object or problem and it can learn how to identify the object or suggest ways to solve the problem. But this only works with very large datasets—not common in knowledge worker domains—and in a very limited set of application areas today.

The answer, though, is not to rail against progress. We should expect employment substitution for some repetitive and routine tasks for most knowledge workers. But we need to examine how we all benefit from the advancements that have been made and concern ourselves with our ability to equip an increasingly aging workforce with skills to thrive in an environment where knowledge and domain expertise matters most. That's the case for Augmented Intelligence today.

We Are Getting Older—And That's Good and Bad

Global aging is unquestionably one of the great success stories in modern society, but it is going to cause a major shift in the workforce and it demands attention and an investment in up-skilling knowledge workers to maintain their relevance and contribute in ways with which they are not experienced or even familiar. Advances in medical science, preventative health care and social care have led to people living much longer lives. Here are some facts:

- By 2050, the world's population over 60 years old is forecast to reach 2 billion.

- In 2016, people aged 65+ outnumber those under 5 for the first time.

- Japan now has a life expectancy at birth of 82 years and this level is at least 79 years in several other developed countries.

- People aged 85 and over (the oldest old) constitute 7% of the world's over-65 population.

- Some countries are experiencing a totally new phenomenon in that the population is both ageing and declining.

A new balance will need to be found between work, retirement and the demographics of those at work. If the world is being shaped by, or solely in the image of, Millennials or the Thumb Generation, problems will occur and opportunities will be missed. We can't ignore the value of hindsight, usually honed by experience and the basis of insight. It is an unfortunate truism that, for many of us, we don't understand the value of experience until we have it. When we do appreciate it, we recognize it as a treasure that we should hold dear and cherish. As knowledge leaves the building there is a risk that the utility of the knowledge workforce is diluted.

The fact is that, as the years progress, fewer younger workers are coming into the workplace. We will need to find a way to make the general labor force, including those over 65, more effective in more value-added knowledge worker roles. Older people, who will otherwise outlive their retirement funds, will need to extend their participation in the economy. This is already happening in some economies. In Japan more than one-third of men over 65 are still economically active, compared to just 2 percent of men in France.

Figure 8: YOUNG CHILDREN AND OLDER PEOPLE AS A PERCENTAGE OF GLOBAL POPULATION: 1950-2050

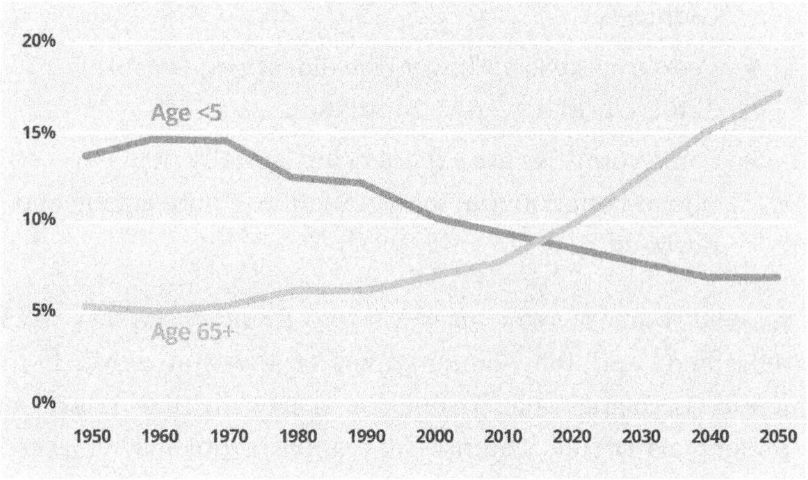

Source: United Nations. World Population Prospects: The 2010 Revision. Available at: http://esa.un.org/unpd/wpp.

In truth, 65 is not old anymore, but for most Baby Boomers—those who were born between 1946 and 1964, and are now between 52 and 70 years old—it has been a long time since they were trained on new skills or learned different approaches that might equip them to perform new roles. There is no physiological reason that many older people cannot participate in the formal workforce. In addition to having acquired more knowledge and job skills through experience than younger workers, older adults show intact learning and thinking. For young and old workers alike, the requirement to up-skill is a certainty. Many jobs will necessitate acquiring new skills to adjust to changing work environments. Businesses or economies that want to achieve that consistently, and at scale, will need to look to technology to fill the knowledge and experience gap.

Augmented Intelligence—a Bicycle for the Mind

In an interview in 1980, Steve Jobs talked about the difference between humans and primates. According to Jobs, the key separation between the two was our ability to build tools that make us more productive. Citing a study that measured the efficiency of locomotion for various species on the planet, Jobs pointed out that the condor used the least energy to move a kilometer, and that humans came in with a rather unimpressive showing, about a third of the way down the list. But, then somebody at *Scientific American* had the insight to test the efficiency of locomotion for a human on a bicycle. And a human on a bicycle blew the condor away, completely off the top of the charts. That was what prompted one of Job's most famous quotes: *"A computer is the equivalent of a bicycle for the mind."*

Augmented Intelligence is today's bicycle, or maybe even today's motorbike, for the mind. It can propel us forward with dignity. It can be pluralistic, caring not about age, gender, or race, but only on how to optimize human potential. That is at the heart of the issue and perhaps one of the key differences between Artificial Intelligence and Augmented Intelligence since this battle of two opposing philosophies has been waged since the 1960s. The proponents of AI propose to confer the machines with *intentionality*. Augmented Intelligence is the idea that a computer system supplements and supports human thinking, analysis, and planning, leaving the *intentionality* to the human.

There is a story told of a conversation between Marvin Minsky, the mathematician who founded AI and who advocates downloading human intelligence, and Doug Englebart, the inventor of word processing, the computer mouse, and hypertext and a strong proponent of Augmented Intelligence.

> MINSKY: We're going to make machines intelligent. We are going to make them conscious!
>
> ENGELBART: You're going to do all that for the machines? What are you going to do for the people?

Englebart reasoned that, because the complexity of the world's problems was increasing, and that any effort to improve the world would require the coordination of groups of people, the most effective way to solve problems was to augment human intelligence and develop ways of building collective intelligence. Through his work at SRI (formerly Stanford Research Institute) in the Augmented Research Center he put forward that the computer, which was at the time thought of only as a tool for automation, would be an essential tool for future knowledge workers to solve such problems.

When Larry Page, one of the founders of Google, was a young graduate student at Stanford, his professor, Terry Winograd, a convert from AI to Augmented Intelligence, counseled him to focus on Web search rather than more esoteric technologies. Page's original PageRank algorithm, the heart of Google's search engine, is the most powerful example of human augmentation in history. The algorithm systematically collected human decisions about the value of information and pooled those decisions to prioritize search results, and then gave it away for free, expanding our potential to self-educate by mining the world's information. Though Google has invested heavily in AI, with the ill-fated Google Glass project and the company's autonomous car developments, it is its search capabilities and Google Maps, another Augmented Intelligence application, that have delivered most benefit to society.

When I think about the role that work plays in people's self-esteem, the prospect of enriching their work experience is appealing. Ignoring or denying the benefits of technological advancements, throwing our hands up in the air in fear of a jobless society where all workers have been supplanted by machines, or disregarding the demographic shifts and our responsibility to respond, leads to a future of poor productivity and in some cases a no-work future—and that strikes me as reckless, depressing and unnecessary.

For knowledge workers there is no scenario where Augmented Intelligence can't help. We don't need the vast datasets afforded to Larry Page to create our own Augmented Intelligence applications. Our ambitions are rarely as grand as Google's mission: *"To Organize the World's Information."* When we apply focus to specific application areas in discrete knowledge domains we can supplement and support human thinking, analysis, and planning, leaving the *intentionality* to the human, just increasing its efficacy.

Augmented Intelligence is the modern-day version of providing a bicycle for the mind, and as we get ready for tomorrow, it can help us to optimize human performance, today.

CHAPTER 3

THE AUGMENTED JOURNEY

Taking the stage at Austin's SXSW festival in March 2016, Chris Urmson, director of Google's self-driving car project, detailed what happened when Google's self-driving Lexus RX 450h crashed into a bus. As documented in the accident report (**Figure 9**), on February 14 in Mountain View, California, a low-speed collision occurred that resulted in minor damage to both bus and car, but no injuries to humans. Google accepted the blame.

> "This is a classic example of the negotiation that's a normal part of driving – we're all trying to predict each other's movements," Google said in its monthly report. "In this case, we clearly bear some responsibility, because if our car hadn't moved there wouldn't have been a collision. That said, our test driver believed the bus was going to slow or stop to allow us to merge into the traffic, and that there would be sufficient space to do that."

It was the first accident caused by one of Google's self-driving cars, despite having already covered 1.4 million miles of real world testing.

Figure 9: DMV REPORT OF A TRAFFIC ACCIDENT INVOLVING AN AUTONOMOUS VEHICLE

DMV
A Public Service Agency

REPORT OF TRAFFIC ACCIDENT INVOLVING
AN AUTONOMOUS VEHICLE

DMV USE ONLY
AVT NUMBER
NAME

Instructions: Please print within the spaces and boxes on this form. If you need to provide additional information on a separate piece of paper(s) or you include a copy of any law enforcement agency report, please check the box to indicate "Additional Information Attached."

- Write unk (for unknown) or none in any space or box when you do not have the information on the other party involved.
- Give insurance information that is complete and which correctly and *fully* identifies the **company** that issued the insurance policy or surety bond, or whether there is a certificate of self-insurance.
- Place the National Association of Insurance Commissioners (NAIC) number for your insurance or Surety Company in the boxes provided. The NAIC number should be located on the proof of insurance provided by you company or you can contact your insurer for that information.
- Identify any person involved in the accident (driver, passenger, bicyclist, pedestrian, etc) that you saw was injured or complained of bodily injury or know to be deceased.
- Record in the PROPERTY DAMAGE line any damage to telephone poles, fences, street signs, guard post, trees, livestock, dogs, buildings, parked vehicles, etc., including a description of the damage.
- Once you have completed this report, please mail to: Department of Motor Vehicles, Occupational Licensing Branch, P.O. Box 932342, MS: L224, Sacramento, CA 94232-3420

SECTION 1 — MANUFACTURER'S INFORMATION

MANUFACTURER'S NAME		AVT NUMBER
Lexus		
BUSINESS NAME		TELEPHONE NUMBER
Google Auto LLC		
STREET ADDRESS	CITY	STATE ZIP CODE

SECTION 2 — ACCIDENT INFORMATION

DATE OF ACCIDENT	TIME OF ACCIDENT	VEHICLE YEAR	MAKE	MODEL
02/14/2016	☐ AM ☑ PM	2012	Lexus	RX450h
LICENSE PLATE NUMBER	VEHICLE IDENTIFICATION NUMBER			STATE VEHICLE IS REGISTERED IN

ADDRESS&LOCATION OF ACCIDENT	CITY	COUNTY	STATE ZIP CODE
El Camino Real and Castro St	Mountain View	Santa Clara	CA 94043

Vehicle was:	☑ Moving ☐ Stopped in Traffic	Involved in the Accident:	☐ Pedestrian ☐ Bicyclist ☐ Other _____	NUMBER OF VEHICLES INVOLVED 1
DRIVER'S FULL NAME (FIRST, MIDDLE, LAST)		DRIVER LICENSE NUMBER		STATE DATE OF BIRTH

INSURANCE COMPANY NAME OR SURETY COMPANY AT TIME OF ACCIDENT	POLICY NUMBER
COMPANY NAIC NUMBER	POLICY PERIOD FROM _____ TO _____

SECTION 3 — OTHER PARTY'S INFORMATION

VEHICLE YEAR	MODEL
2002	New flyer Lowfloor Articulated Bus, series 2300
LICENSE PLATE NUMBER	VEHICLE IDENTIFICATION NUMBER	STATE VEHICLE IS REGISTERED IN

Vehicle was:	☑ Moving ☐ Stopped in Traffic	Involved in the Accident:	☐ Pedestrian ☐ Bicyclist ☐ Other _____	NUMBER OF VEHICLES INVOLVED
DRIVER'S FULL NAME (FIRST, MIDDLE, LAST)		DRIVER LICENSE NUMBER		STATE DATE OF BIRTH

INSURANCE COMPANY NAME OR SURETY COMPANY AT TIME OF ACCIDENT	POLICY NUMBER
COMPANY NAIC NUMBER	POLICY PERIOD FROM _____ TO _____

☐ **Additional information attached.**

OL 315 (NEW 10/2013) WWW

SECTION 4 — INJURY/DEATH, PROPERTY DAMAGE

NAME (FIRST, MIDDLE, LAST)

ADDRESS	CITY		STATE	ZIP CODE

CHECK ALL THAT APPLY ☐ Injured   ☐ Deceased   ☐ Driver   ☐ Passenger   ☐ Bicyclist   ☑ Property

NAME (FIRST, MIDDLE, LAST)

ADDRESS	CITY		STATE	ZIP CODE

CHECK ALL THAT APPLY ☐ Injured   ☐ Deceased   ☐ Driver   ☐ Passenger   ☐ Bicyclist   ☐ Property

PROPERTY DAMAGE

PROPERTY OWNER'S NAME		TELEPHONE NUMBER ( )
STREET ADDRESS	CITY	STATE ZIP CODE
WITNESS NAME		TELEPHONE NUMBER ( )
STREET ADDRESS	CITY	STATE ZIP CODE
WITNESS NAME		TELEPHONE NUMBER ( )
STREET ADDRESS	CITY	STATE ZIP CODE

☐ Additional information attached.

SECTION 5 — ACCIDENT DETAILS - DESCRIPTION

☑ Autonomous Mode   ☐ Conventional Mode

A Google Lexus-model autonomous vehicle ("Google AV") was traveling in autonomous mode eastbound on El Camino Real in Mountain View in the far right-hand lane approaching the Castro St. intersection. As the Google AV approached the intersection, it signaled its intent to make a right turn on red onto Castro St. The Google AV then moved to the right-hand side of the lane to pass traffic in the same lane that was stopped at the intersection and proceeding straight. However, the Google AV had to come to a stop and go around sandbags positioned around a storm drain that were blocking its path. When the light turned green, traffic in the lane continued past the Google AV. After a few cars had passed, the Google AV began to proceed back into the center of the lane to pass the sand bags. A public transit bus was approaching from behind. The Google AV test driver saw the bus approaching in the left side mirror but believed the bus would stop or slow to allow the Google AV to continue. Approximately three seconds later, as the Google AV was reentering the center of the lane it made contact with the side of the bus. The Google AV was operating in autonomous mode and traveling at less than 2 mph, and the bus was travelling at about 15 mph at the time of contact.

The Google AV sustained body damage to the left front fender, the left front wheel and one of its driver's-side sensors. There were no injuries reported at the scene.

☐ Additional information attached.

SECTION 6 — CERTIFICATION

I certify (or declare) under penalty of perjury under the laws of the State of California that the foregoing is true and correct.

I further certify that I am the authorized Administrator of the program for the above named employer.

PROGRAM DIRECTOR/AUTHORIZED REPRESENTATIVE PRINTED NAME AND TITLE	TELEPHONE NUMBER
CHRIS URMSON , DIRECTOR	
SIGNATURE X	DATE SIGNED 2/23/16

OL 316 (NEW XI/2013) WWW

Urmson explained that the company had taught its cars to move next to the curb when planning a right turn, sidling by traffic stopped at a traffic light, much as human drivers do. As the car proceeded along the curb, it sensed a few sandbags on the road ahead of it, so decided to stop and wait for the lane next to it to clear. After the light turned green, the traffic began moving. The car detected a city bus coming up the lane, and made the assumption the bus driver would slow down. As Urmson told it, the bus driver assumed the car would stay put, and kept on going. The car pulled out, hitting the side of the bus at about 2 mph. The experience of the car involved in this collision was captured as a new set of driving parameters for every other car in Google's fleet.

Figure 10: THE EASY-MILE SELF-DRIVING BUS

Google is at the forefront of the autonomous car movement, but it is not on its own in facing the challenge to prove that self-driving vehicles can share the roads safely with human drivers. In the summer of 2016, in the Hernesaari district in Helsinki, Finland, in a limited real-world trial, two EasyMile self-driving buses are already taking passengers to their destinations, albeit at speeds limited to just over 6 mph. Finland is one of the first countries to try out the minibuses on city roads, thanks to its laws allowing cars to roam without a driver. In April 2016 Dubai also signed a deal with the company to test the EasyMile vehicles, while in August 2016 a Japanese mall began using them to shuttle shoppers around.

Automakers like Tesla, Toyota, Nissan, Audi and BMW are all racing to hit the streets with their own self-driving vehicles. The Obama administration got behind the efforts to bring driverless vehicles to US roads and has committed $4 billion to that goal—which includes attempts to develop standardized regulations for autonomous cars across the entire country. The efforts of the National Highway Traffic Safety Administration (NHTSA) are noteworthy also and the NHTSA has defined five levels of autonomy based on how many car functions are computer-controlled.

Figure 11: NHTSA's FIVE LEVELS OF AUTONOMY FOR AUTONOMOUS VEHICLES

	LEVEL 0 1972 Chevrolet Vega	LEVEL 1 1998 Mercedes S500	LEVEL 2 2016 Tesla Model S	LEVEL 3 Uber, Google	LEVEL 4 JohnnyCab from *Total Recall*
Driver	Life is a highway—the driver is in complete control of the care at all times	Driver can regain control or stop the car more quickly than when driving without the automated function or functions	Driver shares control as an intermittent operator; you'll want to take your hands off the wheel, but you shouldn't	Professionally trained operator for ride-hailing service cedes full control during certain conditions	Driver selects destination, doesn't control car functions
			Partial automation of at least two primary control functions working together (e.g. adaptive cruise control with lane centering) to relieve driver of the tasks	Steering, throttle, braking, and other critical functions are automated; the car can monitor changes in road conditions (e.g., construction) that might require the human to retake control	Fully automated; designed to perform all safety-critical functions and monitor road conditions for an entire trip; responsibility for safe operation rests solely with the vehicle
Vehicle	Automatic transmission optional	Automation of one or more specific control functions, such as assisted braking			

Graphic by Bloomberg Businessweek Data, Completed by Bloomberg

In May 2016, the first autonomous vehicle-related fatality occurred. The crash involved a 40-year-old Ohio man who was killed when his 2015 Tesla Model S drove under the trailer of an 18-wheeler on a highway near Williston, Florida. Tesla's Autopilot capability—though never billed as autonomous and only as augmented capability for the driver—did not notice the white side of a tractor-trailer against a brightly-lit sky. Similar issues highlighting the limitations of machine vision when compared with the capability of the human eye, such as driving in snow or very bright light, are an as yet unsolved set of challenges for the autonomous vehicle community.

Knowledge and Humans

The initial Google crash and the more tragic Tesla crash both highlight two areas of concern for self-driving vehicles: How do such cars navigate situations that typically require human instinct? And who's to blame when a self-driving car gets into an accident with a human-driven car: the human, or the company that built the software?

The answer to the second question, *"Who's to blame?"* is fraught with complexity and philosophical opinion. To answer it will require the changing of minds, and the opening of minds, and the combined efforts of governments, insurance companies, technology and automotive companies, and consumer protection agencies to resolve, and that will take a while.

The first question, *"How do such cars navigate situations that typically require human instinct?"* is somewhat more tractable. It highlights two core tenets of Augmented Intelligence that underlines its greater efficacy and practical potential when compared with the common vision of AI. These are *knowledge* and *humans*.

Let's look at what Chris Urmson from Google said when he was describing what happened in that Valentine's Day crash. He said that **the company had taught its cars to move next to the curb when planning a right turn, sidling by traffic stopped at a traffic light, much as human drivers do.** The key phrases here are *"the company had taught"* and *"much as human drivers do."* Before Google taught the cars what humans do, it could not even conceive of putting a driver-less or human-less car on the road. It had to teach the car about safe braking distances, to look in the rearview mirror, to understand stop-lights, to assess the relative speed of other vehicles in its surroundings, to recognize when a pedestrian stepped out in front of the car, to ignore the bird flying overhead, to know where there were one-way streets, to avoid construction work on the road, *much as human drivers do*. This need for a deep foundation of knowledge, in the particular domain to which the application is being deployed, is a concept that is not sufficiently understood when people talk about AI or Augmented Intelligence applications.

The problem for the self-driving car movement is a need for perfection. Unlike smartphones, virtual reality, and basically any other big Silicon Valley-based push of the last decade, autonomous vehicles can't be an ongoing experiment for consumers. We've become accustomed to beta tests and frequent software updates—using technology in its nascent stages and watching as it evolves over time. However, by the time everyday drivers begin taking their hands off the wheel and their foot off the pedal, the technology cannot afford to fail.

In a debate on this topic at SXSW, David Strickland, a former NHTSA Administrator, who oversaw the first policy statement from the NHTSA on autonomous testing on public roads said, *"For there to be consumer acceptance of these vehicles, they have to be virtually perfect."*

Stepping through the five levels of autonomy for driverless cars as defined by the NHTSA (**Figure 11 above**), we can see that the human involvement needed at each level diminishes in direct correlation to the level of knowledge built into the car. But until we get to Level 4, the fictional JohnnyCab from *Total Recall*, we can see that the human is still involved—and, for now at least, JohnnyCab is still a Hollywood invention that only has to work on the big screen and not in the real world.

Where experience matters, as it does for many scenarios in the world and for knowledge workers in business, the greater the initial foundation of knowledge and context-awareness, the less likely it will be that the system will make an erroneous judgment. If the application domain being addressed requires judgment or creativity, the efficacy of the applied reasoning in the context-aware application will be much greater if the application is infused with knowledge. But there still needs to be a facility for the human to intervene as required to correct the outcome or to augment the knowledge in the system.

The Confluence of Augmentation

Google's competition in autonomous cars may not come from the traditional automotive sector, though we know that every car manufacturer is investing heavily in this area. The challenge is more likely to come from Tesla in a small way, or

Apple in a big way. The most likely outcome is perhaps a combination of the two, if Apple goes ahead and buys Tesla.

The Apple Car is in the early stages of development. In September 2015 it was upgraded to 'committed project' status, meaning it's getting even more attention and hiring for the project is expanding to 1,800 employees. Under the new leadership of Bob Mansfield—a senior long-term Apple executive, who took over in July 2016—Apple's focus now is more on autonomous driving systems. That will perhaps allow it to partner with or purchase a car manufacturer in the future. Apple is now said to be pursuing a two-prong development approach—**working both on a car and the software to power it**—and anticipated delivery is now 2020 or 2021.

With Siri, Apple already provides one of the world's most-used narrow AI applications. Through the acquisition of VocalIQ and Perceptio in October 2015, Siri should get smarter in the short term. With the acquisition of Seattle-based Turi in August 2016, the company is further bolstering its Machine Learning and AI capabilities. The battle of the AI giants 'Google v Apple' is now heating up. But there is also a smaller company in the wings.

"Uber-izing" the World

Near the end of 2014, the CEO of Uber, Travis Kalanick, flew to Pittsburgh on a mission: to hire dozens of the world's experts in autonomous vehicles. The city is home to Carnegie Mellon University's robotics department, which has produced many of the biggest names in the newly hot field. Sebastian Thrun, the creator of Google's self-driving car project, spent seven years researching autonomous robots at CMU, and Chris Urmson was a CMU grad student.

Kalanick is known for being ambitious and aggressive in pursuit of his goals. In August 2016 Uber introduced a fleet of driverless cars to downtown Pittsburgh, allowing customers to summon self-driving cars from their phones. Customers will request cars the normal way, *via* Uber's app, and will be paired with a driverless car at random. In the first instance, humans in the driver's seat will supervise Uber's Pittsburgh fleet. Trips were planned to be free during the initial trial period.

"The minute it was clear to us that our friends in Mountain View [Google] were going to be getting in the ride-sharing space, we needed to make sure there is an alternative [self-driving car]," says Kalanick. *"Because if there is not, we're not going to have any business."* Developing an autonomous vehicle, he adds, *"is basically existential for us."*

In July 2016 Uber reached an agreement to buy Otto, a 91-employee driverless truck startup. Otto has developed a kit that allows big-rig trucks to steer themselves on highways, in theory freeing up the driver to nap in the back of the cabin. The driverless trucks will be used to start an Uber-like service for long-haul trucking. The Otto deal is a coup for Uber in its battle with Google, which has been plotting its own ride-sharing service using self-driving cars. Otto's founders were key members of Google's operation who departed from Google in January 2016. Google suffered another setback in August 2016 when Chris Urmson announced that he, too, was leaving.

Kalanick believes that Uber can use the data collected from its app, where human drivers and riders are logging roughly 100 million miles per day, to quickly improve its self-driving mapping and navigation systems. That gets to the heart of Google Maps—probably the world's favorite Augmented Intelligence application.

Google Maps and Augmented Intelligence

About a billion people every month, who between them conduct about a billion searches every day, use Google Maps. It is now so ubiquitous, such a vital part of so many of our lives, that it feels odd to think it didn't exist until 2005. Of all of the search giant's many tentacles reaching octopus-like into every area of our existence, Maps, together with its partner Google Earth and their various offspring, can probably claim to be the one that has changed our day-to-day life the most.

For most people, how Google Maps works is not understood. From their perspective, the application just works and, like any good Augmented Intelligence application, that's how it should be. But a tremendous amount of innovation and investment has gone into making the complex task of providing directions from one location to another so simple to use. It is a wonderful example of how humans have poured oceans of knowledge into a system to make other humans more productive. The maps we used to keep folded in the glove compartments of our cars were a collection of lines and shapes that we overlaid with human intelligence. Now, as we've seen, a map is a collection of lines and shapes with embedded knowledge and intelligence.

Behind every Google Map, there is a much more complex map that's the key to your queries but hidden from your view. The deep map contains the logic of places: their no-left-turns and freeway on-ramps, speed limits and traffic conditions. Google, which began as a search company, figured out that, as the mobile world exploded, *where* you were searching *from* became as important as what you're searching *for*.

Google Maps began as a desktop program designed by Where2 Technologies. In October 2004, Where2 was acquired by Google and together they converted it to a web application. Where2 was a tiny startup based in Australia that almost went bust before the Google deal. Just before Where2 expected to finalize an agreement with Sequoia Capital, Sequoia dropped funding discussions with them when Yahoo Maps launched an update that added Yellow Pages entries on a map.

Through a series of other acquisitions and licensing agreements Google added a host of knowledge sources to the maps. Notable acquisitions were Keyhole, a geospatial visualization company, and Zipdash, a company that provided real-time traffic analysis. Zipdash was a lot like Waze, a company that Google acquired in 2013 for $1 billion (a lot more than the $2 million that CEO Mark Crady received for Zipdash). Mapping data from Tele Atlas, a Netherlands-based mapping company, and a host of other data services were also included.

In 2007, TomTom bought Tele Atlas and Nokia bought Navteq, and so Google initiated a project—called Ground Truth—to control its own map data. A team of 20 people across the world worked full-time on acquiring map data. Megan Quinn (now General Partner at Spark Capital), who led the data acquisition project, sent out an email to every Google employee asking them to find inaccuracies or bugs in the maps for their home towns, promising them a home-made cookie for every bug they found. Quinn ended up baking

7,000 chocolate-chip cookies. This was a critical wave of human input to Google Maps.

The sheer amount of human effort that goes into Google's maps is just mind-boggling. Google understands that the best way to figure out if you can make a left turn at a particular intersection is still to have a person look at a sign—whether that's a human driving or a human looking at an image generated by a Street View car. Humans are coding every bit of the logic of the road onto a representation of the world so that computers can simply duplicate (infinitely, instantly) the judgments that a person already made.

Knowledge, Data, Context, Reasoning, and Notifications

Next time that you are standing on the sidewalk in Manhattan looking for directions to your meeting on the Upper East Side, sitting in your car in Sausalito thinking about a trip to Monterey, or if you are a little more adventurous, planning to explore the Angkor Wat UNESCO world heritage site in Cambodia, or heading out from Helsinki on a trek to see the Northern Lights from Pitkäjärvi Lake in Finland, you can use Google Maps to plot your course. It's all because Google has made the investment to infuse Maps with a ginormous foundation of knowledge, much of it collected through automation, but quite a bit of it augmented by human input and ingenuity.

Google Maps is the most wonderful example of an Augmented Intelligence application. We all understand it. Although the task of mapping the world is on a scale that dwarfs any business application, Maps clearly contains all of the components that should be on your list if you are building an augmented application for knowledge workers.

I split my time between traveling in the United States and living in Cork in Ireland. I am a very keen, but very bad and infrequent, golfer. When I have American visitors to my home in Cork, I recommend taking a trip to Waterville Golf Club in the extreme South West of Ireland. Even if you are not a golfer, the trip to Waterville is stunningly beautiful and shows off the best of Ireland, particularly when it is not raining. When I can I drive my guests to Waterville myself, but if I don't have the time, I just use my iPhone to show them how to find this gem of a destination for themselves. Using all of the Augmented Intelligence capabilities in Google Maps my friends can confidently head off on their trip.

Figure 12: GOOGLE MAPS: CORK TO WATERVILLE

It starts with **Knowledge**. Because Google has effectively mapped the world, it has a foundation of knowledge with which it can work to build the journey plan. Then we key in **Data**: our chosen destination 'Waterville Golf Links.' As

Google Maps has geo-location services built in, it does not need to be told the starting location. It has the **Context**. Now it begins its **Reasoning**. Because I live in a neighborhood that has only one way out to the main road, it tells us to make a U-turn if the car is facing the wrong direction. As we are in Ireland, Google knows that we should drive on the left-hand side of the road and when we encounter a roundabout it knows that we should navigate it in a clockwise direction.

As you can see from the map, the trip takes a little over two and a half hours. Along the way, as the location or Context changes, the user is continuously receiving **Notifications**, pushing information to the driver in plenty of time for the driver to know the next action to take: *"In 500m, at the roundabout take the second exit and continue on the R641"*.

How Google Maps works provides us with a blueprint for Augmented Intelligence applications in business and in the next chapter I will describe some examples. Knowledge, Data, Context, and Reasoning are critical components of these or any Augmented Intelligence applications for knowledge workers. Where updates occur in any of Knowledge, Data, or Context, then Notifications are needed to keep the user in the loop on anything that might impact the situation.

Augmented Intelligence applications need to have knowledge of the core concepts of the specific domain to which the application is being applied. Experienced practitioners and domain experts know the 'How to,' the 'Best way,' the proven approaches to solving the problem and getting to a specific solution destination. Making that available to someone who is making that journey for the first time by providing signposts—effectively a map of the journey—means it is less likely that they will take a wrong turn. Knowledge on its own is not enough; Data and Context are necessary. Without Context, it is really hard to apply the knowledge and, without Data, you don't know the specific problem you are trying to solve.

Augmented Intelligence applications make the journey of knowledge workers more frictionless, and make it easier for less experienced workers to add more value to their companies and to get more satisfaction from the work that they do. It starts one journey at time and gets more valuable with each human interaction to uncover new destinations and greater possibilities.

Without Google Maps, or similar technology, autonomous cars would not be possible. We wouldn't have Uber, or Lyft, or any other service that depends on geo-location services, and we would still be struggling to fold up the paper map to fit it back into the glove compartment in our cars. Those days are better left behind.

CHAPTER 4

AUGMENTED INTELLIGENCE FOR KNOWLEDGE WORKERS

With the introduction of Augmented Intelligence platforms for knowledge workers, we can evolve. We can deliver real value, we can enlighten our employees and customers, and we can be there to augment their understanding of the problems they are trying to solve. That is what will consistently drive optimal outcomes. Instead of 'Artificial' Intelligence, the real-world work of business is Augmented Intelligence—and its benefits for knowledge workers will be extraordinary.

In this chapter, using the enterprise sales profession as a proxy for all knowledge workers, I am going to describe how Augmented Intelligence can be applied to a specific business domain. The enterprise salesperson represents one of the most knowledge dependent professions, where, while every journey is different, the map to success, though extremely complex, is still materially the same—from one journey to the next. Imagine if sales professionals had the muscle memory of a million sales engagements, represented as a multi-dimensional map, sitting on their phones, right beside Google

Maps. They will surely be likely to get to their chosen destination—a closed sale or growing account—much more frequently. That is achievable through Augmented Intelligence today and I will describe an example later in this chapter.

The 800-pound Gorilla in the sales productivity market today is undoubtedly Salesforce. Through the extraordinary vision of its founder, Marc Benioff, the cloud computing industry in business has evolved to be one of the core future trends that we all should care about. Could Salesforce be the Google of knowledge workers, providing the Augmented Intelligence equivalent of Google Maps? Is there an app for that? With the August 2016 announcement of Salesforce Einstein, to be launched at the company's Dreamforce event in October (after this book will be published), this may well be the platform for Salesforce and its partners to bring AI, in its many forms, to the broader business world.

When you look at the profile of Salesforce's customers, you see knowledge workers. You see people whose mental acuity, experience and knowledge are the ingredients that, when fresh and invigorated, deliver a recipe for success. These are the knowledge workers who drive successful businesses forwards, who think for a living. The anatomy of the Salesforce ecosystem suggests that it is from here that the democratization of Augmented Intelligence might emerge. But first I want to revisit the concept of the knowledge worker and the knowledge economy.

Thinking for a Living

Knowledge worker is not a new concept. Peter Drucker, the Austrian-born American management consultant, educator, and author first coined the term 'knowledge worker' in 1957. According to Drucker, *"the most valuable asset of a 21st-century institution, whether business or non-business, will be its knowledge workers and their productivity."* Drucker knew little about Augmented Intelligence, but he understood, probably better than most, the value and importance of the knowledge economy and the demands that it placed on modern companies.

Alvin Toffler was an associate editor at *Fortune* magazine. He argued that the consequence of 'information overload' in society and the accelerated rate of technological and social change left people disconnected. He captured those thoughts in his book, *Future Shock*, a seminal publication that went on to sell 6 million copies. In 1990, Toffler observed that typical knowledge workers in the age of the knowledge economy must have some system at their disposal to create, process and enhance their own knowledge. He too foretold the need for Augmented Intelligence.

In 1991 Ikujiro Nonaka, a Japanese organizational theorist and Professor Emeritus at Hitotsubashi University, described knowledge as the fuel for innovation, but was concerned that many managers failed to understand how knowledge could be leveraged. Nonaka advocated a view of knowledge as renewable and changing, and that knowledge workers are the agents for that change. Nonaka highlighted one of the key challenges in Augmented Intelligence—the ever-changing nature of knowledge.

Let's consider the observations on knowledge workers from these three legendary thinkers:

- **Drucker**: The most valuable asset of a 21st-century institution, whether business or non-business, will be its knowledge workers and their productivity.

- **Toffler**: Knowledge workers in the age of the knowledge economy must have some system at their disposal to create, process and enhance their own knowledge.

- **Nonaka**: Managers failed to understand how knowledge could be leveraged … knowledge workers are the agents for that change.

These comments were made before the recent advancements in Augmented Intelligence systems, and, even without the knowledge of the advantages that such systems could bring, Drucker, Toffler and Nonaka foretold the need. Knowledge workers are the fuel that powers the engine of the modern business. Enhancing the productivity of knowledge workers is the ultimate competitive advantage for business.

If you are reading this, you are probably a knowledge worker—someone who thinks for a living. Your busiest day of the week is probably a Tuesday (see **Figure 13**). You might be a software engineer, business analyst, pharmacist, consultant, architect, sales person, engineer, marketer, scientist, public accountant, or lawyer. Fundamentally though, your job is to "think for a living."

The Salesforce Economy

As a knowledge worker, you're through most of your planning for the week on Monday, then Tuesday to Thursday are busy and generally pretty productive, before things begin to ease off on Friday, before tailing off dramatically for the weekend. At least that's the picture painted by those who connect to Salesforce's systems, most of whom are knowledge workers. Salesforce serves more knowledge workers with enterprise business applications in the cloud than any other company. (*Note:* **Figure 13** is in reverse date order from left to right—August 20, on the extreme left, is a Saturday, and time moves backwards to July 19, a Tuesday, as you move right along the chart.)

**Figure 13: SALESFORCE DAILY TRANSACTION VOLUME—
TUESDAY IS ALMOST ALWAYS BUSIEST**

Salesforce, self-styled as *The Customer Company*—"We make your customers love you"—began life in 1999 as a software-as-a-service (SaaS) company, providing sales force automation software. Marc Benioff (a former executive from Oracle), Parker Harris, Dave Moellenhoff and Frank Dominguez founded the company. Harris and his team wrote the initial sales automation software, which launched to its first customers in the fall of 1999. Though the bulk of the company's annual $8 billion revenue still comes from its flagship Sales Cloud product, in the financial quarter ending April 30, 2016, 41% of revenue came from Sales Cloud, 31% from Service Cloud, 18% from App Cloud and 10% from Marketing Cloud—it has extended the scope of its offerings to cover most application areas for knowledge workers. Salesforce is the company that has had most impact on the growth of cloud computing in business.

According to the company's website:

> Salesforce is the world's #1 CRM company. Our industry-leading Customer Success Platform has become the world's leading enterprise cloud ecosystem. Industries and companies of all sizes can connect to their customers in a whole new way using the latest innovations in cloud, social, mobile and data science technologies with the Customer Success Platform.

In August 2016, Salesforce paid $750 million to acquire Quip. Crunchbase describes Quip as *"a living document platform that combines docs, spreadsheets, and communication,"* but it is really Salesforce's answer to Office365 from Microsoft. Strengthened by the Microsoft 2016 acquisition of LinkedIn, where the Redmond-based company beat the San Francisco-based company into second place, Microsoft has become the only plausible competitor to Salesforce in the Customer Relationship Management (CRM) market as evidenced by its placement on the Gartner Magic Quadrant.

Salesforce appears to be fighting back with Quip and going after the heart of Microsoft's business: the knowledge worker in the office, who will be a core beneficiary of Augmented Intelligence.

As of August 2016, Salesforce had not yet announced what Quip will be called when integrated into the Salesforce product suite, but I would not be surprised to see it named Office Cloud (unless this violates Microsoft's trademarks) or Productivity Cloud. In any case, Salesforce, clearly the enterprise cloud leader, is going after the knowledge workers in the cloud-enabled enterprise by providing an alternative to Microsoft's Office 365, to grow or defend its CRM core business. I can't get inside Benioff's head but I might surmise that will be to gain more mindshare from the knowledge worker. Both Microsoft and Salesforce, of course, also have Google Docs to contend with—not an insignificant competitor for Quip or Office 365 or indeed for anything related to AI.

While it is a minnow in comparison with the Internet giants—Amazon, Alphabet (formerly Google), Facebook, and the other technology titans Apple and Microsoft—**Salesforce is the company best positioned to deliver Augmented Intelligence solutions for knowledge workers**. It has the reach, the breadth of applications, a scale of daily transactions—at more than 4 billion transactions per day—data traffic, and signal inputs to be able to begin to emulate Google Maps' behavior in the context of business. To date, however, with the exception of RelateIQ, most of Salesforce's efforts in intelligence have been centered on its acquisitions of predictive or data analysis technologies (see **Figure 14**).

The difference between Salesforce and the aforementioned Internet giants is that, for today at least, Salesforce is focused solely on business, not consumer applications. Over its 17 years in business it has developed a deep understanding of the breadth of application needs of its customers. With its own offerings for Sales, Marketing, Service, Analytics, Platform and Apps, and IoT (Internet of Things), Salesforce can solve a lot of problems for its customers.

Figure 14: SALESFORCE's AI-RELATED ACQUISITIONS

- **BeyondCore**, August 2016—Smart Data Discovery technology gives users a full range of descriptive, diagnostic, predictive and prescriptive bias-free analytics.
- **Coolan**, July 2016—Leverages Machine Learning to provide peer benchmarking and historical data that predicts failure trends, prevents outages, and informs purchasing decisions.
- **Implisit**, May 2016—Leverages predictive analytics to boost sales organizations' performance and revenue.
- **Metamind**, April 2016—Automatic image recognition powered by artificial intelligence.
- **PredictionIO**, February 2016—Open source Machine Learning server.
- **MinHash**, December 2015—Brings the power of artificial intelligence to uncover emerging trends that are relevant and actionable.
- **TempoAI**, May 2015—Tempo Smart Calendar, a mobile productivity app that organizes the user's day.
- **RelateIQ**, July 2014—A relationship intelligence platform that allows teams to track, share and analyze professional relationships.
- **Prior Knowledge**, September 2011—Goes beyond traditional Big Data Analytics by learning the deep structure of data and generating predictions that reflect all of these relationships.

Descriptions by Crunchbase.

I am not one to bet against Salesforce or the vision of Marc Benioff, but to fully serve the knowledge workers in the companies that are its customers, Salesforce needs to provide an AI platform capability for its customers and partners to infuse domain-specific knowledge into the Salesforce platform. This may well be the vision for Salesforce Einstein announced in August 2016 and billed as the world's first comprehensive AI for CRM. As the company integrates the technologies from its AI-related acquisitions it will have to enable not just AI applications, but hopefully Augmented Intelligence applications as well. Salesforce has both the ingredients and the opportunity.

As can be seen from the description on the company website, Salesforce is also *"the world's leading enterprise cloud ecosystem."* Salesforce recognizes that it can't serve all needs on its own. That's where AppExchange comes in. Launched in 2005, the Salesforce AppExchange is an online application marketplace for partner applications that run on the Force.com platform. With more than 3,000 applications and 4 million application installs, AppExchange is the most successful business cloud application marketplace in the world. It validates Salesforce's claim to be the world's leading enterprise cloud ecosystem, and it provides over 1,000 Salesforce partners with a platform to build innovative applications in the cloud to serve different business needs of Salesforce customers.

Now with Salesforce Einstein, this is where it gets very exciting in the context of AI, particularly the Augmented Intelligence variety. I see a future where the Salesforce AppExchange is augmented to become the Salesforce Knowledge Exchange, where its partners—who specialize in business areas that Salesforce itself does not serve—can bring domain-specific knowledge to the market that leverages the Salesforce Einstein platform.

Altify Max—Augmented Intelligence on Salesforce

One of Salesforce's partners is Altify,[5] whose primary purpose in life is to improve performance and productivity for sales professionals, sales managers, and executive sales leadership in companies that sell complex business applications to business enterprises. Founded by a team with heritage in AI, sales methodology and enterprise cloud applications, the company provides a range of intelligent software applications on the Salesforce platform that guides sales people to win sales opportunities, increase revenue from large customers, and maximize the effectiveness of a sales organization. In April 2016, through its research and knowledge arm, the company announced Altify Max, an Augmented Intelligence platform for Sales.

The sales professional, particularly the sales professional involved in complex enterprise selling, is the poster child for the knowledge worker. Like many other knowledge workers, enterprise salespeople do not produce anything physical. They think for a living, and the quality of that thought, the foundation of knowledge on which the thinking is based, the context and timeliness of their actions, and the data they use to formulate their sales strategies are the core ingredients that predict success. The team behind Max focused initially on the enterprise selling domain, an area in which the company had particular domain expertise, given that it was the day-to-day focus of its business.

---

[5]   The author is Altify's CEO.

> If Google Maps can provide directions to guide salespeople to meetings with their customers, shouldn't there be an Augmented Intelligence application that helps them to navigate all the twists and turns in the road to winning a sale.

Throughout the 1980s and right up to the present day, companies have invested heavily in training their sales teams on how to be more effective in enterprise selling. Most of these companies, like Miller Heiman, Sales Performance International, and CEB are deep in knowledge, but light on automation, and all lack any kind of intelligent software support. According to ATD, the market for sales training and sales methodology in 2015 was $20 billion but, although there was typically a high quality of knowledge disseminated in the classroom or online through eLearning, the efficacy of the training was sub-optimal. This is because there has been no effective technology deployed to operationalize the new way of working that adoption of the sales methodologies would require. Given that most of the companies did not have a technology background, this is not overly surprising. Building enterprise-class software is not a trivial task.

From 2013 to 2016 venture capital firms invested large amounts of capital in lots of companies that targeted the sales performance market with product offerings using AI or Predictive Analytics. These companies provided the technology but did not have the core knowledge of the sales methodologies. The problem with the 'knowledge-less' AI in most black-box sales solutions is that the black-box doesn't 'understand' complex enterprise sales, and reductive pattern-matching or Machine Learning on its own oversimplifies, and can actually impair, progress.

Applying 'Big Data' techniques to enterprise sales doesn't work well. Enterprise sales is a Small Data problem, not a Big Data problem. There is not enough consistent data for an individual sales person to draw accurate conclusions from patterns — and the individual seller is a key variable. So, the Machine Learning approach outlined in **Chapter 8** will not work on its own. There is not enough homogenous training data for the machine to learn. Secondly, as we know, any functioning AI system must first be taught the intelligence and the knowledge. It can't learn the basics on its own. If Google Maps did not have maps with knowledge of all the places in the world on which to base its routing algorithms, it could not give you directions. It is the same in enterprise sales. You need a map or a blueprint to start with. The problem, therefore, that the Max team set out to solve was to provide a framework that could infuse an application with enough knowledge to guide the sales person on how to avoid a mistake in a sales process and plot the course for success.

The Inner Workings of the Max Project

In the previous chapter, using Google Maps as an example, I listed the core components of an Augmented Intelligence application: Knowledge, Data, Context, Reasoning and Notifications. Each of these apply equally well in Augmented Intelligence applications for knowledge workers. The Max approach could be applied to any domain area but, sticking to the axiom of narrow domain specificity for effective Augmented Intelligence applications, the focus initially was on the Sales domain and specifically the various sales personas. Altify had acquired a sales methodology business a number of years prior to this project, so the team had great access to domain expertise. That solved the Knowledge problem.

Joe the Salesperson—Joe is working a sales opportunity, Max monitors the critical data and events in the deal. When something of importance happens, Max assesses the impact, notifies Joe of the need to act, and prescribes the action Joe should take to progress the opportunity.

Figure 15: MOBILE MAX

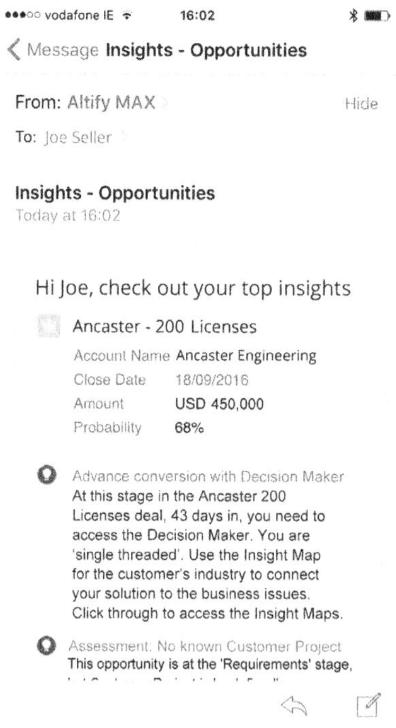

Laura the Sales Manager—As Laura is busy managing her sales team, Max is keeping an eye on her sales forecast, her pipeline and her team's key deals. Max notifies her to schedule a deal review for an important deal to keep it on track, or points out when her sales forecast is at risk and recommends corrective action.

Max instantly identifies warning signs, and notifies Laura so that she can mitigate risk earlier in the sales process.

> **Sales Forecast Risk: Large deal ($450,000) needs attention.**
> Your sales forecast for the quarter has increased by $200,000 but the level of risk has increased. Joe Johnson's Ancaster Engineering opportunity has increased from $250,000 to $450,000, but this is more than 3 times the average deal size for Joe Johnson. There are 62 days remaining in the quarter. That is 52% of their average sales cycle. The opportunity is at Requirements stage in the funnel. Access to the buyers looks weak. There is a good understanding of the business problem. No decision criteria have been identified. Click here to schedule a deal review with Joe Johnson.

Ken in Sales Operations—Ken, informed by Max, sees opportunities to improve the team's performance. Using the Max Insight Editor (**Figure 16**), Ken can enhance the knowledge in Max to provide smarter guidance to the sales team to proactively and consistently get better results. Ken can tailor Max to his unique business and sales process by customizing or extending the supplied knowledge and insights.

There can be hundreds of moving parts in a long, complex enterprise business sale. Max could now analyze the data in Salesforce, and the inputs to other applications in the Altify Platform, to allow the sales person to make the most informed decision possible, while coaching them with prescribed guidance on what they should do next. The Max team examined all of the data gathered by the CRM and Altify platforms and reduced it to a set of **Insight Signals** on which Max could act.

In complex enterprise sales environments, there are many different considerations that determine the likelihood of winning a deal:

- The customer's urgency to act.
- The degree to which the seller is engaged with the decision-makers.
- Budget allocation or access to funds for a purchase.
- How well the seller's product addresses the customer's needs.
- The relative preference of the buyer for a particular solution.
- The level of risk perceived by the customer.
- Whether the seller is selling a proven or new product.
- The degree to which a solution is differentiated from the competition.
- Whether the buyer is from an existing or new customer.
- The speed at which the sale is moving through the sales process.

Each of these considerations, and many others, were coded into Max as Insight Signals and made available to the domain experts to build **Insights**. Insights are the directions or guidance that the salesperson needs to take the next action to progress the sale. The Max team and the domain experts, both within Altify and within the early customers, reported that the catalyst for creating impactful Insights was the Max Insight Editor capability (**Figure 16**).

Once the Insight Signals had been created, the domain experts could iteratively and incrementally pour knowledge into the system. Then they would test the Insights against a representative set of sales opportunities to see what advice would be presented to the salesperson in different situations. In its first release Max contained 50 core Insight Signals and 200 Insights that catered for the most common twists and turns in an enterprise sale. Many more have since been added.

FIGURE 16: MAX INSIGHT EDITOR—RULES, ADVICE AND CONTEXT EDITED IN A SIMPLE GUI

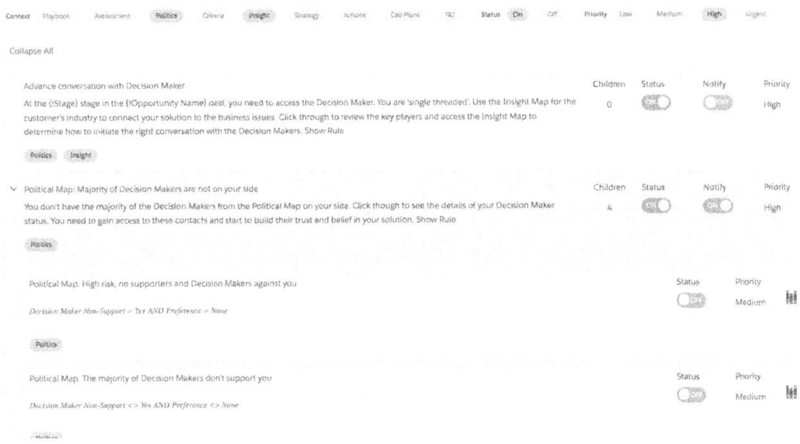

Situations always change in sales and Max has to cater for the fact that the advice provided has to change based on the **Context** of a sale. If a salesperson, working on a large sales opportunity in their Salesforce CRM, suggests that the opportunity is in the final stage of the sales process, or in the last sales pipeline stage, but that key decision-makers have not yet been identified, then Max can highlight the vulnerability and advise on actions that the salesperson might take to progress the deal or re-evaluate the situation. That advice would not be relevant or appropriate for new sales opportunities where the salesperson may not have had the time yet to uncover information about the decision-makers.

Also, depending on the size of the sales opportunity, various sales channels, or the geographic location of the salesperson or customer, different Insights would be more or less applicable.

The Max team developed a general-purpose expert system rules engine on the Salesforce platform to conduct the **Reasoning** on the Insight Signals. In a similar way to Google Maps, Max would look at where the sales person was at any point in a sales process. It always understands the destination—the salesperson is trying to win the deal. Then Max plots a map to get from here to there. Using all of the knowledge that has been built into the system, time and time again Max would identify risks and vulnerabilities in sales opportunities that many sellers would miss. In the first release of Max, it provided **Notifications** through email, Salesforce Chatter, and directly within the Opportunity Record on the Salesforce system (**Figure 17**), where the salesperson would go to add and update details of their deal.

A lot of thought and effort went into the logic for Notifications. The team recognized that they needed to ensure that every time the seller received a notification it would not be unduly repetitive, it would relate only to the few most important and urgent opportunities and it would be immediately actionable from the notification itself.

One of the crucial components of Max that received a lot of attention was the Max Insight Editor (see **Figure 16**). Having identified the importance of knowledge expansion and Reciprocal Data Application (RDA) capabilities, heavy investment was made to provide non-technical users in customer organizations with a facility to modify or expand the Insight Signals and Insights.

Figure 17: MAX IN A SALESFORCE OPPORTUNITY RECORD

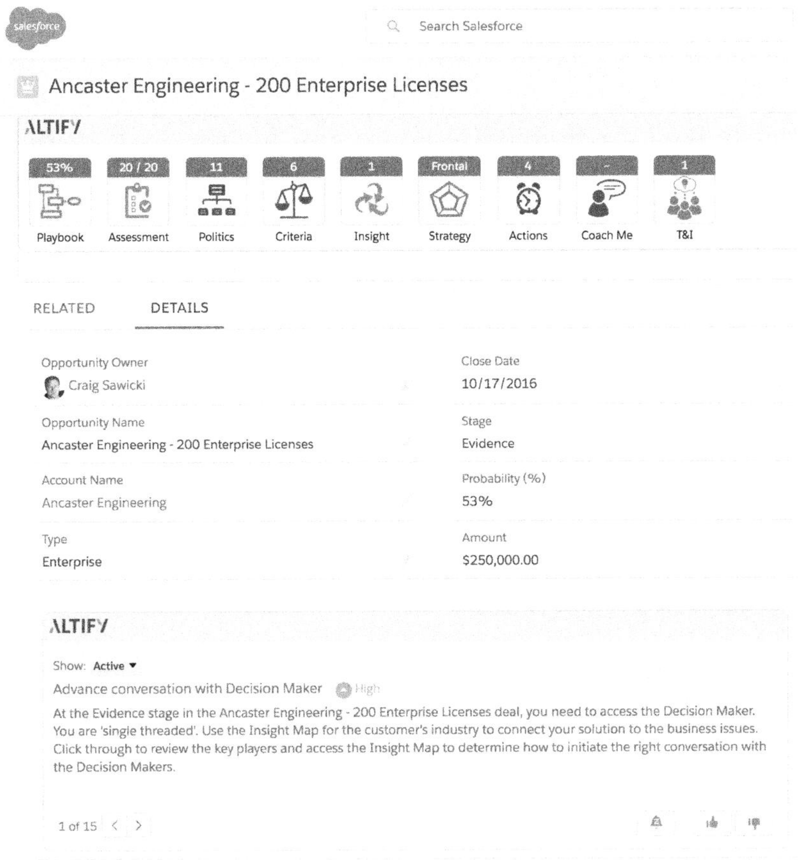

In **Chapter 8**, RDA capabilities will be discussed in the context of Machine Learning. This is where applications are designed to encourage users to help teach the machine. In Augmented Intelligence applications a similar concept must be applied to blend human knowledge and decision-making expertise, *via* small amounts of data with a feedback loop akin to the Human-in-the-Loop (HITL) construct that will be explained in **Chapter 9**.

Building this into Max reduced dependency on the project team to be the sole source of knowledge and so the companies that use the system have the ability to build their own industry-specific knowledge into their instance of the application.

The final step in the initial Max project was to close the loop. The team built a learning engine to measure the efficacy of the Augmented Intelligence application as applied in each scenario (**Figure 18**). If Max could highlight which Insights were most frequently relevant, it could deduce competency gaps. Measuring how often a user engaged with each Insight, either by acting on it directly or by 'liking' it in the same way that they like a post on Facebook, Max could infer which Insights were deemed to deliver most value. By measuring the impact on a sale from each Insight that was used by the users, Max could distil the most valuable Insights from the rest and guide the domain experts to refine and improve the efficacy of the system.

Figure 18: ALTIFY MAX: AUGMENTED INTELLIGENCE INSIGHT ENGINE

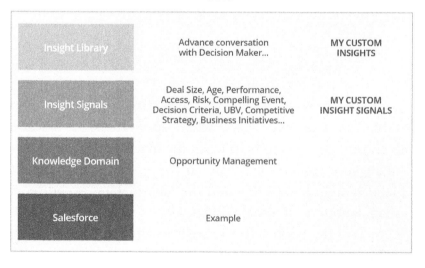

Closing The Loop

Altify Max is one example of an Augmented Intelligence platform for knowledge workers. It enables domain experts and knowledge workers to define Insight Signals and Insights, so that with applied knowledge, it can be turned into competitive advantage and business value. The word 'platform' is important. Much more than simply a faster and cheaper way to enable knowledge workers to more effectively perform, the Max platform is a new model for creating and distributing Augmented Intelligence, and it is built in the cloud, native on the Salesforce platform. Now with Salesforce Einstein, Max will likely be able to leverage a much broader set of Insight Signals.

The Altify Max team has also proven that Max works in a broader set of domains, not just sales, though they are looking to partners to provide the domain expertise in those areas. With any data in Salesforce, the partners, or Salesforce customers themselves, can select a knowledge domain, and build Insights and Insights Signals. That will allow them to provide an Augmented Intelligence application that can add value to the knowledge workers in their company.

As I wrote at the outset, with the introduction of Augmented Intelligence platforms for knowledge workers, we can evolve, we can deliver real value, we can enlighten our employees and customers, and we can be there to augment their understanding of the problems they are trying to solve. That is what will consistently drive optimal outcomes. As you have just seen, instead of 'Artificial' Intelligence, the real-world work of business is Augmented Intelligence—and its benefits for knowledge workers will be extraordinary.

CHAPTER 5

THE BIG DATA CONUNDRUM

Where Big Data Fits in AI

It is hard to think about AI, whether that means Artificial Intelligence or Augmented Intelligence, without thinking about the data behind the machine. In general commentary, we see terms intermingled; Machine Learning, Big Data, Analytics, and Artificial or Augmented Intelligence are blended in a futuristic soup of technology bits and bytes, signals and noise.

Deloitte, the global business management consulting firm, released a report in July 2016 entitled *Analytics Trends 2016 — The Next Evolution*. The report highlights what the authors view as six key emerging trends. The first: *The man-machine dichotomy blurs.*

Are machines coming for us?

The newsstand rhetoric posits that smart machines will soon take over our jobs. Fear not—there's still a place for us. Humans have always added value to machines as processes become automated, and this is likely to continue. Still, the cognitive age is clearly upon us, as indicated by more than $1 billion in venture capital funding for cognitive technologies in 2014 and 2015.

Analysts project that overall market revenue for cognitive solutions will exceed $60 billion by 2025. As cognitive technology evolves, it is likely to become just another tool in the toolbox—a very useful for the right application but not replacing traditional analytics capabilities that also complement the human thought process. The man-machine dichotomy is not "either-or." It is unequivocally "both-and."

You could be forgiven for thinking that the Deloitte report is about Artificial Intelligence or Augmented Intelligence as described earlier in this book, not about Analytics *per se*. But they are connected. As you have wandered through the book, you will possibly have found yourself wondering where is the separation between Machine Learning, Big Data, Analytics, and AI (Artificial or Augmented). This confusion is one of the barriers that we have to overcome to enable leaders in business, the knowledge workers who think for a living, to understand how to best use these exciting technologies to propel their business forward. These discrete technologies converge in certain cases for large complex applications but diverge on axes of both complexity and utility, depending on the scenario at hand.

Machine Learning can't happen efficaciously without Big Data and Analytics—but Analytics can certainly exist without ML. AI applications without very large data and a tsunami of input will not be very intelligent at all, but by creating a foundation for the application that is based on knowledge, Augmented Intelligence can be very effective for knowledge workers. To bridge the dichotomy, we should appreciate that this—our future lives shaped by the evolution of technology—is a question of horses for courses. We want to be sure we are riding the right horse for the right course, and to know when the horse should be a machine, or whether the horse should be a human. Context, scale, and application domain, are vectors that we can use to consider our position, the magnitude and complexity of the task and the path or journey we should take. Big Data is valuable—but like AI, it is not the panacea that some of the marketing hyperbole would suggest.

The Big Data Thing is Big. It's Very Big

Many years ago, I scraped together all my pennies to buy my first house. I was about 24 years old. I was very proud walking in the door of my new home. I walked around the empty rooms pinching myself to be sure that it wasn't a dream—I had actually managed to become a property owner. Well, of course, the bank really owned the house—all I really owned was the mortgage—but that wasn't how I thought about it then. It was all good, except of course for the fact that the rooms were empty. Having made the down payment on the house I didn't have any money left to furnish it. But that wasn't the biggest problem for me.

You see, I'm a very big music fan. As I'm writing this I have *The Loud Hailer*, the new Jeff Beck album, playing in the background. As I meandered through my new house, when I should have been freaking out about the paint peeling off the walls and the malfunctioning heating system, instead I was worried that since I had now moved out of my parents' house I didn't have a music system—we used to call it a 'HiFi' system back then—to play my large collection of vinyl records. I didn't have a TV or microwave either, but I could survive without those. How would I get by if I couldn't listen to music? In the end I managed to convince my older brother, also a big music fan, to give me a loan. I remember sitting on a very old couch that had been left in the house by the previous owner listening to *The Nightfly* from Donald Fagen (of Steely Dan fame), reading the cover notes, and watching the album spinning on the turntable. Bliss!

How things have changed. Imagine how I would address that problem today. As long as I could get access to a WiFi network (surely I could cajole the neighbors to give me access to their network if I couldn't afford one of my own—though I can't imagine not having WiFi connectivity as the first must-have in any house move), Spotify, YouTube, or Pandora would come to my rescue. My vinyl record collection, or at least its contents, has now been replaced by digital notes in the cloud, clustering to form chords and harmonies. In fact, many of the physical artifacts of my youth have been replaced by a digital *doppelganger*. No more celluloid or physical photoprints; digital cameras and smartphones capture the images, and iPhoto, Flikr, or Picasa store the photos so I can access them whenever I want, anywhere in the world. Gone from my life are phone books, paper diaries, and print newspapers. I don't have a Rolodex or address book on my desk. I don't send bound copies of monthly reports or company presentations; I just share a link to Dropbox. I can't remember when I last saw, let alone used, a fax machine. You're probably reading this book on your Kindle, iPad or laptop, unless I sent you a hard copy of the book.

Many goods that used to be physical in the past are digital now, and every time you tap, click, pinch or swipe, data is captured and becomes part of the Big Data mountain in the sky. If you underline a sentence in this book while reading it on your Kindle, I will know. I won't know that it is *you*, but I will know the sentences that are most frequently underlined.

Amazon captures that. If you purchased this book on Amazon, you will also have seen *"People who buy this, also bought that."* Every interaction is being measured. If you bought a hardcopy book, then every step in the journey from Amazon to FedEx, to your house, has been tracked, recorded and analyzed so that Amazon can tell you how long it will take for you to get the next book you buy. More signals, more data, more noise. When physical things become digital things they become data elements in their own right, casting a digital shadow and spewing digital exhaust as they go on their journey—more noise and data pollution in the network. The amount of data being created is so vast that the value of data is diluted.

What Data Matters?

The economic rules have changed in the digital economy. The 'Cost of Goods' in a digital world is a fraction of the physical equivalent. The physical cost of making a digital copy of this book for everyone on the planet is almost zero. So we tend towards making more, logging more, tracking more—filling data centers with noise as we follow a mantra of *more data is better.*

According to an August 2016 article in *Forbes* magazine, *Roundup of Analytics, Big Data & BI Forecasts and Market Estimates, 2016,* investment in Big Data is continuing to grow are a staggering pace:

- **Gartner:** Global revenue in the Business Intelligence and Analytics market is forecast to reach $16.9 billion in 2016, an increase of 5.2% from 2015.

- **IDC:** Big Data and Business Analytics worldwide revenues will grow from nearly $122 billion in 2015 to more than $187 billion in 2019.

- **Wikibon:** Global Big Data market will grow from $18.3 billion in 2014 to $92.2 billion by 2026.

- **451 Research:** The Total Data market is expected to nearly double in size, growing from $69.6 billion in revenue in 2015 to $132.3 billion in 2020.

- **Marketresearch.com:** Global Business Intelligence and Analytics software market is expected to increase from $17.9 billion in 2014 to $26.78 billion in 2019.

- According to **Stratistics Market Research Consulting,** the Big Data Analytics & Hadoop market accounted for $8.48 billion in 2015 and is expected to reach $99.31 billion by 2022.

I could give you more data—there are lots more forecasts and predictions—but I don't think that it would help. While there is clearly a lot of money being invested today, and Big Data plays an important role in some businesses, it is hard to know how big it is going to get. There is very considerable variance in the predictions. We can only assume that the research companies involved are reporting on different things. The big questions—as is often the case with data—are: "*What are we measuring? What data matters?*" There is too much Big Data, but not enough big questions.

To try to make sense of these forecasts, I created a table that plotted the starting and ending forecasts from each of the firm's data, and put them on a timeline from 2014, the first year for which we had a starting point, and 2026 (!) the last year for which we had a prediction (**Table 1**).

Table 1: BIG DATA FORECASTS 2014–2026 (US$ billion)

Research Company	2014	2015	2016	2017	2018	2019	2020	2021	2022	...	2026
Gartner		16	17								
IDC		122				187					
Wikibon	18										92
451 Research		70					132				
Market Research	18					28					
Stratistics		9							99		

Next, I wanted to fill out the picture. Using the start and end market size data from each prediction as seed data for my calculations, I calculated a reverse CAGR (compound annual growth rate) from the data provided by each of the research companies, making an assumption that the CAGR would not change over the period. You can see that the CAGR ranges from 5.2% to 40.86%.

Table 2: FORECAST CAGR

Research Company	CAGR
Gartner	5.20%
IDC	11.27%
Wikibon	14.56%
451 Research	11.15%
Market Research	9.24%
Stratistics	40.86%

I then extrapolated the data forwards and backwards as necessary to fill out the table.

Table 3: BIG DATA FORECASTS 2014–2026 ($ billion) WITH CAGR

Research Company	2014	2015	2016	2017	2018	2019	2020	2021	2022	2023	2024	2025	2026
Gartner	15	**16**	**17**	18	19	20	21	22	23	24	25	27	28
IDC	106	**122**	136	151	168	**187**	208	232	258	287	319	355	395
Wikibon	**18**	21	24	28	32	36	41	47	54	62	71	82	**92**
451 Research	63	**70**	77	86	96	106	**132**	147	163	181	201	224	249
Market Research	**18**	20	21	23	25	**28**	30	33	36	40	43	47	52
Stratistics	6	**9**	12	17	24	33	47	66	**99**	140	197	278	391

The point of this exercise is not to try to get an accurate prediction of the Big Data market for the next 10 years—it could be $28 billion or $391 billion! I think it is impossible to do that with any degree of certainty, but I went through this example to reflect on the problem with looking at non-homogenous data sets. Even in this small sample, there are too many unknowns, too many variables and too much subjectivity for the inferences to be reliable. This is not an uncommon problem—particularly when dealing with domain areas where we are not using large datasets. Even when we have the luxury of large datasets, we still need to know the questions to ask, and then consider the *"So what?"*

In another market prediction, Gartner says that the CRM market will be $36.5 billion in 2017, with ERP at $34.4 billion and BI at $18.6 billion. So, which should you care about most? It clearly depends on your perspective and the context of our business.

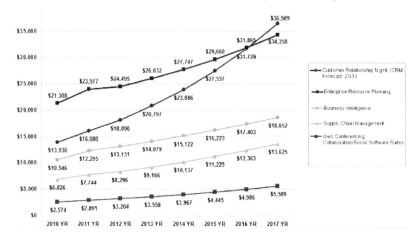

Figure 19: WORLDWIDE ENTERPRISE SOFTWARE REVENUE BY SUBSEGMENT 2010–2017 (US$ million)

There is clearly a lot going on in Big Data. According to Firstmark Capital, Big Data startups received $6.64 billion in venture capital investment in 2015. That's about 11% of total VC investment in technology in 2015. And there are good and bad stories out there.

My fear is that we are trying to make business more data-focused instead of making data more business-focused.

As Adam Leary, lead data scientist and senior director of the data team at CBS Interactive, says:

> The hype has been around not only the amount of data but also around the idea that data can solve all your problems. Vendors have come to us and said, "You can build all these dashboards, and now you have insights." Well, you don't really have insights if the team doesn't know what their own goals are, right? You can provide them with amazing outputs, but if you really don't know how to make it part of your own goals, if you don't have the level of sophistication to use it, you're going to miss out. That's a big organizational culture question. Analytics can help you

a lot, even give you a competitive advantage, but only if you know how to use it.

Do I Need Big Data, or Just Analytics?

Here's where I need to distinguish between Big Data and Analytics, and to try to get beneath any confusion in the market. In some commentaries they are used interchangeably, or referred to as Big Data Analytics as a single phrase, and these unclear monikers contribute to the mess. We don't all need Big Data, but most of us in business need some form of Analytics. You can benefit from Analytics without using Big Data, but you can't benefit from Big Data if you don't have Analytics.

Gartner defines Big Data as data that exhibit three particular attributes:

- High **volume**.
- High **velocity**.
- High **variety**.

So, you've a lot of data that is coming at you fast, from many different sources, in many distinct digital formats. In addition to Gartner's Volume, Velocity and Variety, I have also seen Veracity added to the Big Data definition. I don't believe that Veracity—the quality of the data—is solely the preserve of Big Data though. Whether I am using an Excel spreadsheet or a Salesforce dashboard to analyze just a few thousand records, if the data doesn't reflect the truth, the analysis is of little value.

Let's look at these four attributes in more detail:

- **Volume**: An example of Big Data volume will certainly exceed terabytes and might be petabytes (1,024 terabytes) or exabytes (1,024 petabytes) of data consisting of billions to trillions of records of millions of people —all from different sources (Web, sales, customer contact center, social media, mobile data and so on).

- **Velocity**: Think of a firehose of data, or a constant data stream that is changing constantly and at a rapid pace. Processing 1GB of data per day can get you to Big Data volumes in few years.

- **Variety**: Big Data means much more than rows and columns; it means a range of data types and sources that might include unstructured text, video, audio or images.

- **Veracity:** Driven by the quality of the data you collect and the amount of computing (not human) horsepower it might take to normalize / remediate it.

These four vectors are not benefits. They are **problems**. You should not go looking for a Big Data solution unless you are experiencing at least two of these problems. Don't go searching for more data so that you can then solve the Volume problem or Variety problem. Big Data is always challenging and costly. Resources invested in data management are not available for analysis, or action, so Big Data may not be a blessing.

For the most part, Big Data projects live in IT, are managed by data scientists, who in conjunction with the rest of the business, have figured out what data is important, what questions need to be answered, and how that analysis will be used to effectively drive the business forward. The majority of knowledge workers are recipients of the output of Big Data projects but most are not actively involved in them. That should not be the case with Analytics. In fact, for most knowledge workers you may not need Big Data at all.

Some problems are quite complex, but that doesn't mean they need Big Data quantities of data. Let's assume for a moment that you are a rocket scientist working on a manned space mission. Your data needs (according to an old NASA manual) will include:

- Astronauts' physical condition and medical information.
- Geodesy (spacecraft location) and gravitational fields.
- Meteorology—cloud cover and radiation balance.
- Atmospheric physics.
- Air density from drag and non-gravitation forces.
- Ionospheric physics.
- Magnetic fields.
- Cosmic rays and trapped radiation.
- Electromagnetic radiation (UV, X-ray and gamma).
- Interplanetary medium (the material that fills the Solar System).

Seems like a lot of information. According to Lucy Simon Rakov, one of the programmers from the Mercury Project, the first United States' manned space program, the computers used on that project offered a whopping 300 kilobytes of memory. That's *kilobytes*! Not exa-, not peta-, not even mega-, but kilobytes.

You can do a lot with a small amount of data, and you don't even have to be a rocket scientist.

Know What Data (and Analytics) You Need

Unless you're already making very good use of ordinary, small-scale data in your work, you're not ready for Big Data right now and you probably don't need it. Chances are you just need to start using data, period—or make better use of what you have.

The challenge for many companies is that they struggle to use the data that they already have. They create lots of reports, sometimes add visualizations, and still fail to gain any insight from their data. Companies don't magically develop those competencies just because they've invested in high-end Analytics tools. The answer is not in data size, but in practice and principles.

To a computer, of course, practice and principles have to be taught, and for a report to deliver useful insight through analytics it needs to understand the nuance and relationships in the data, and the potential path to patterns. But here's the key: humans, in comparison, are far better at the art of being curious, asking questions and knowing what questions to ask. That's at the heart of good Analytics (and indeed Big Data as well). More often than not, that is why the real value of the data surfaces when the humans set the stage for the questions, the interpretation and the analysis.

The purpose of Big Data and Analytics is to help accelerate decision-making and to increase the quality of the decision. Fast data is better than Big Data. *"We have let ourselves become enchanted by Big Data only because we exoticize technology,"* Peter Thiel says in his book, *Zero to One: Notes on Startups, or How to Build the Future.* But we needn't be overawed or dazzled by Big Data. There are ways we can sift through this information and impact our business decisions for a good outcome.

Specifically, businesses will gain more advantage from data by taking these four steps:

1. Understand the four types or phases of Data Analytics:

   o Descriptive.

   o Diagnostic.

   o Predictive

   o Prescriptive.

2. Focus on smaller, more actionable datasets.

3. Put the Analytics tools in the hands of the knowledge workers themselves to shorten the time to value.

4. Add a little Augmented Intelligence.

These steps, and a few other things, are the focus of the next chapter.

CHAPTER 6

AUGMENTED ANALYTICS

At various points in our lives, or on a quest, and for reasons that often remain obscure, we are driven to make decisions which prove with hindsight to be loaded with meaning. – **Swami Satchidananda**, *The Yoga Sutras*

Hindsight, Insight and Foresight

A little bit of insight at the moment of truth—the trigger point in a decision cycle—is considerably more valuable than all of the data or information in the world 24 hours after the trigger point event. If I know, after the event, that I made the wrong decision, there is not a lot that I can do to change the outcome. In the absence of a modified DeLorean car with Marty McFly at the steering wheel, as we saw in the 1985 movie *Back to the Future*, I can't go back in time and change my decision. Fast matters.

A directionally correct insight delivered on time is better than the perfect insight delivered late. The purpose of Analytics for knowledge workers should be to serve up the 'almost perfect' insight fast, in advance of the trigger point event, to provide some foresight into consequences of different decisions so that the decision made is both informed and timely.

Figure 20: HINDSIGHT, INSIGHT AND FORESIGHT

Hindsight	Looking back at the data, with an informed perspective based on domain expertise.
Insight	Applying knowledge, experience, to know what the data means so that you can interpret the results
Foresight	Being able to predict outcomes and prescribe remedial action where necessary

As we have progressed over the recent decade, and started to get benefit from the available technologies, most companies are at a point where they have a pretty good idea of what has happened in the past, assuming that the data recorded is both complete and accurate. Hindsight is, after all, 20:20. Economists are really good at hindsight, but are the poster children for horribly inaccurate forecasts.

In a January 2016 article in *The Financial Times*, glowingly entitled *An Astonishing Record—of Complete Failure*, Prakash Loungani, an economist with the International Monetary Fund wrote, *"The record of failure to predict recessions is virtually unblemished."* The record of failure remains impressive. There were 77 countries under consideration in the forecasts Loungani examined, and 49 of them were in recession in 2009. Economists—as reflected in the averages published in a report called *Consensus Forecasts*—had not called a single one of these recessions by April 2008.

The economy is a notoriously complex beast and there are just so many factors to consider that getting it right can reasonably be considered hard. The recurrent theme that emerges from researchers who examine the inaccuracy of economists' forecasts is that the lack of insight into the current state—a blind belief that what happened in the past will just repeat itself—leads to the lack of foresight, and consequently any forecast that they come up with is not even directionally accurate. Economists have to make forward-looking statements using only a rearview mirror. No wonder it is hard for them to see.

In business, predicting a sales forecast is also notoriously inaccurate. To say that forecasting is the bane of existence of most sales managers and leaders is probably a bit of an understatement. It is estimated that forecast accuracy in most sales organizations runs at about 50%—just half of the sales opportunities that are forecasted to close do so as projected. Might as well flip a coin.

Similar to the economists' problem, there is usually a lot of historical data from sales managers to work with. But while the hindsight that the data provides can be a guide at a macro-level, it is rarely sufficiently useful when applied to an individual sales opportunity because it is lacking contextual insight. Also, many sales processes have been designed by the selling organization to map to their selling activities rather than to the customer's buying activities and many times these two are out of sync. In fact, all along the way, in the buying cycle, the customer is making a series of micro-decisions as a guide to the right purchase decision. Often the sales process does not reflect the actions that would need to be taken to guide the buyer to make a favorable micro-decision. No insight, no foresight.

This is where applied experience is a lot more valuable in Analytics than many people realize. It is certainly more important than raw data, and requires different parts of the brain to figure out. A good designer of an Analytics model is curious, and that curiosity can find nuances in historical data, which when viewed through the eyes of experience, and enriched by the insight garnered through deep contextual knowledge, can join the dots so that the Analytics model itself is infused with insight and can deliver foresight to the human on the other side of the computer screen.

Data and the Four Stages of Analytics

We are moving to a point in the development of technology where we have transitioned from a stage where we were learning how to use a computer to one where we are helping the computer to learn about us. As we deploy Analytics to help solve business problems, we should consider how much context we can teach the computer so that it can notify us to take the appropriate action when necessary.

> Don't measure anything unless the data helps you make a better decision or change your actions. If you're not prepared to change your diet or your workouts, don't get on the scale. – **Seth Godin**

Data without action is just data and has little value. Data is not actionable on its own. A human with the requisite domain knowledge can look at data and figure out what to do with it, but a system does not know this on its own unless we build in this ability. The system does not automatically know that the data is meaningful. With all of the power available to us today with Analytics systems, at the end of the day, if it processes a bunch of data and tells me that the average revenue I can get from all of my customers is $100,000, but a particular customer that I am interacting with has the potential to grow to $300,000, then it needs also to tell me what I should do about it. On its own, and in many Analytics implementations today, the system does not automatically notify people who need to know the insight that it has just uncovered. It does not recognize that we need to do something about it.

The answer is making that data actionable. That is about engagement. We want the system to:

- Understand the data from the past—Descriptive Analytics.

- Deduce from that data the key signals that correlate to changes in outcome—Diagnostic Analytics.

- Predict what will happen (based on current context)— Predictive Analytics.

- Recommend actions using Prescriptive Analytics.

Now *that* is effective engagement, the apogee of good Analytics implementations. This is Augmented Analytics because it is guided by humans and processed by machines.

There are many definitions for each of the terms 'Descriptive Analytics,' 'Diagnostic Analytics,' 'Predictive Analytics,' and 'Prescriptive Analytics' that are generally similar but with enough variances that it is worth defining what I mean by each term. My definitions generally line up with those you will find in Gartner's *Glossary*, and that's as good a reference point for my reading audience as any.

According to Gartner, **Descriptive Analytics** is the examination of data or content, usually manually performed, to answer the question *"What happened?"* (or *"What is happening?"*), characterized by traditional Business Intelligence and visualizations such as pie charts, bar charts, line graphs, tables, or generated narratives. We all do a lot of this in reports and dashboards in the CRM. But, let's face it, very few people enjoy poring over reports trying to figure out what it all means, particularly if they were not involved in the design of the report, and so don't have an understanding of why the report was created in the first place. Dashboards, or other visualizations, are one step up the ladder, but if we are to empower the knowledge worker, we don't want to have to teach them how to interpret the charts.

Diagnostic Analytics helps you to understand why something happened and, more importantly, what data matters. Gartner's *Glossary* entry for Diagnostic Analytics is:

> A form of advanced analytics which examines data or content to answer the question "Why did it happen?" and is characterized by techniques such as drill-down, data discovery, data mining and correlations.

For me, the clue is in the name: Diagnostics Analytics summarizes raw data into Insight Signals that are interpretable by humans.

However, Diagnostic Analytics are not usually well instrumented, and analytics and interpretation cycles are wasted on spurious and often erroneous predictions. Deriving those Insight Signals is a core foundation to the following Predictive Analytics and Prescriptive Analytics, because without knowing which signals 'move the needle' it is impossible to predict what might happen or to prescribe what you should do about it. Diagnostic analysis can help avoid the correlation *versus* causation mistake.

Correlation *versus* Causation

Two events can consistently correlate to each other but not have any causal relationship. An example is the relationship between reading ability and shoe size across the whole population of the United States. If someone performed such a survey, they would find that larger shoe sizes correlate with better reading ability, but this does not mean large feet cause good reading skills. Instead it's caused by the fact that young children have small feet and have not yet (or have only recently) been taught to read. In this case, the two variables are more accurately correlated with a third: age.

The part age plays in this example is known as a confounding variable or confounding factor and is something that is not being controlled for in the experiment. In this case, age influences both reading ability and shoe size quite directly. A confounding variable can be the actual cause of a correlation; hence analysis must take these into account and find ways of dealing with them, usually by searching them out and trying to alter this variable directly.

Correlation does not imply causation, but it does waggle its eyebrows suggestively and gesture furtively while whispering, *"Look over there."* Correlation, if disconnected from causation, is usually a distraction.

Data and the Four Stages of Analytics (continued)

If we know why something happened in the past, the theory goes that we will have a better chance of figuring out what will happen next. **Predictive Analytics** help you to understand the future. Gartner says:

> Predictive Analytics is a form of advanced analytics which examines data or content to answer the question "What is going to happen?" or more precisely, "What is likely to happen?" and is characterized by techniques such as regression analysis, multivariate statistics, pattern matching, predictive modeling, and forecasting.

Predictive Analytics provides companies with insights on what might happen in the future. It is important to remember that no statistical algorithm can 'predict' the future with 100% certainty. Companies use these statistics to forecast what might happen in the future.

The rapidly evolving **Prescriptive Analytics** capability allow users to 'prescribe' a number of different possible actions to take. In a nut-shell, these analytics are all about providing advice on *"What to do next?"* Gartner's take:

> Prescriptive Analytics is a form of advanced analytics which examines data or content to answer the question "What should be done?" or "What can we do to make ___ happen?"

Prescriptive Analytics build on Predictive Analytics. In addition to the prediction of what will happen, Prescriptive also suggests actions you can take to take advantage of the predictions, by recommending one or more possible courses of action.

Figure 21: DATA AND THE FOUR STAGES OF ANALYTICS

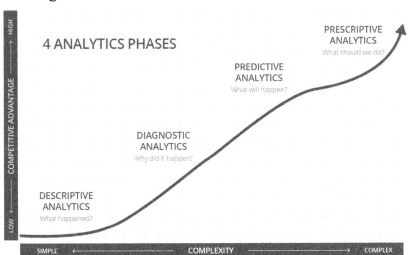

Avoiding the Pitfalls—Plugging the Gaps with Humans

Many organizations that are investing heavily in Analytics, and hiring data scientists to slice and dice the data, appear frustrated. They undeniably have more data that they had before, and in most cases (because there has been a focus on the data) the quality has improved. The data scientists and software tools are rarely a significant cause of the frustration, but they find themselves spending more time and money while failing to garner significantly better insight.

Now that technological advances have made it possible to accumulate colossal amounts of data at an increasing rate, it has become almost axiomatic that the answer to everything is in the data. But, in fact, it is not. Companies are making big bets on Big Data and Analytics—Big Data Analytics (!)—without the qualitative assessment that is required to apply deep domain expertise. That has the potential to lead to big decisions being made with misplaced confidence. Here are some guidelines to avoid the most common pitfalls.

> Advances are made by Answering Questions. Discoveries are made by Questioning Answers. – **Bernard Haisch**

1. Starting with Questions

One of the most common misunderstandings about Analytics is that, if you look at data hard enough, you will find insights. Staring at daily dashboards in the hope that insights will miraculously reveal themselves is often overwhelming, confusing and unsuccessful.

Successful Analytics start by identifying the question you're trying to answer from the data. For example, if website conversion—enticing the user to take a specific call-to-action from your website—is an issue, instead of studying your website data hoping to find reasons for low conversion, narrow down your efforts to a specific question. In this case, it might be: *"What are the leading indicators that we should measure in the website traffic that can help us to increase conversions from 23% to 26%?"* This approach allows you to focus on finding actionable drivers of conversion that can have impact.

Another question that might be used by a sales manager who wants to increase revenue in his sales team is: *"What can the data tell me about the average value of each sales opportunity that we work, the win rate for each member of my team, and how long it normally takes us to win a sale?"*

These are things that all sales managers want to know and using hypotheses to narrow the data set needed generates secondary questions to further refine the insights, such as: *"When we win a deal, how often have we engaged with all of the customer's key decision-makers?"* or *"What are the attributes of customers who have most frequently purchased Product X?"* or *"Of all the sales opportunities that we pursue, are we winning the larger or smaller deals?"*

The primary hurdle that people have to overcome is how to know what questions to ask. That is more of a heuristic experience-based challenge than it is a pattern recognition or data analysis problem.

What do you want to know? Why do you want to know it? What will you do with the answers? These are all good questions to start with.

2. It's About the Business, Not (Just) the Science

Analytics for knowledge workers is about knowledge. Analytics should not be viewed as an IT project, but as a business project, focused on a narrow domain area—bigger is not always better—to help the knowledge workers in the business to better perform the tasks they have to execute every day. Without the right business context, it is hard to know what questions to ask—so, in that case, any answer should do—but, of course, that doesn't work. It is understandable, though that, if there is too much of a separation between the people with the business knowledge and the people with the Analytics tools, then success is less likely. This is because a tool is just a tool and if you don't have business expertise, domain knowledge, experience and a 'nose' for what's right then you can't apply any human qualitative input—and that makes it hard to connect the dots.

What are the important business outcomes that you want to impact? The answer to that should drive your Analytics focus. You might start with the Key Performance Indicators in your business and work back from there.

If a manufacturing professional needs to increase the throughput from his manufacturing plant, he will probably want to look at the amount of product produced (per machine, shift, operator). But he will also likely examine Reject Ratio, Machine and Process Speeds, Production against Target, Task Time, Machine Utilization, Overall Equipment Effectiveness and Downtime. These are not new concepts to manufacturing professionals, who for years have been using some mix of Kaizen, Lean, Six Sigma, and TQM to help improve processes—but Analytics can help to deliver greater insight when they start with the right questions, informed by their business experience.

3. And Then There Was Light—Building Trust

It's extraordinarily hard for people to change from making decisions based on personal experience to making them from data—especially when that data counters the prevailing common wisdom. But upsetting the *status quo* is much easier when everyone can see how it could contribute to a major goal. With a potential big reward in sight, a significant effort is easier to justify, and people across functions and levels are better able to support it.

"How can we reduce the sales cycle for our enterprise deals?" *"What changes do we need to make to ensure that the deals we focus on and forecast, are actually the ones that we can win—in line with the forecasted size and timeline?"* If you focus on the benefit that such insights would deliver, you have a better chance of getting people on board with the project in the first instance.

Figure 22: AND GOD SAID …

… *and God said:*

$$\nabla \cdot \mathbf{D} = \rho$$

$$\nabla \cdot \mathbf{B} = 0$$

$$\nabla \times \mathbf{E} = -\frac{\partial \mathbf{B}}{\partial t}$$

$$\nabla \times \mathbf{H} = \mathbf{J} + \frac{\partial \mathbf{D}}{\partial t}$$

… *and then there was light*

Science is increasingly answering questions that used to be the province of religion. – **Stephen Hawking**

Equally importantly, though, is the need to build trust in the outputs, the insights, the predictions and the prescriptions. If one of your quantitative experts develops an ingenious algorithm that pulled in all pipeline and sales data, historical sales forecasts and actual results, to suggest future sales behavior, the system should also explain the 'why' behind the recommendations. For the users to trust the algorithm and the results it promises, they have to understand, in so far as is possible, the sequence of 'thinking' that was used to derive the result. I call this the 'Thinking Chain.'

Here is an example of a Prescriptive Analytics notification and the associated thinking chain:

> **Sales Forecast Risk: Large deal ($450,000) needs attention.**
> Your sales forecast for the quarter has increased by $200,000 but the level of risk has increased. Joe Johnson's Ancaster Engineering opportunity has increased from $250,000 to $450,000, but this is more than 3 times the average deal size for Joe Johnson. There are 62 days remaining in the quarter. That is 52% of their average sales cycle. The opportunity is at Requirements stage in the funnel. Access to the buyers looks weak. There is a good understanding of the business problem. No decision criteria have been identified. Click here to schedule a deal review with Joe Johnson.

The final step in building trust is to close the loop. Allow users to give feedback on the insight or advice by using something akin to a Facebook 'Like' to indicate if they found the insight useful.

It is equally important to measure the efficacy of each insight. Which insights were presented most frequently, and what measurable difference occurred when the insight was acted upon? As your project progresses you will learn about which insights the users think are most valuable and which are actually moving the needle in your business. Bring your users on this journey. It will help you to build a foundation of trust, a prerequisite for any effective organizational change.

4. Objectivity and Confirmation Bias

The purpose of any analysis should be to get to the objective truth, the insights that will allow you to determine the actual factors that drive the results, rather than spurious correlations that might lead you to specious predictions.

Once you have uncovered those deterministic factors you can begin to develop some heuristics or rules of thumb that are based on experience and are empirically true. These rules must pass the *"Do I believe it?"* test. Using commonsense — which unfortunately is not necessarily all that common when faced with copious amounts of seemingly correlated data — you can test your assumptions to develop a meaningful prediction or forecast in a systematic way rather than on an *ad hoc* basis.

Assiduous application of this approach will get to a level of accuracy that is much greater than average and will trend towards higher precision over time. Of course, there will always be exceptions, situations that you have not considered or experienced in the past and being open to this possibility will improve the way you assess the results of your analysis. Always question and focus on the rules or process being applied. Sometimes you will get it wrong, but that's OK. Rather than being disappointed in getting it wrong, you can rightly be pleased that you have got it as right as you could. While it may seem counterintuitive, the paradox is that, by focusing more on the process than on the results, you are more likely to get better results.

When something doesn't fit into our established way of thinking we usually blame the something instead of questioning our way of thinking. Trying to fit a square peg into a round hole, you might blame the peg, when maybe the problem is with the hole. So, when the results of your

Analytics efforts result in an outcome that you didn't expect, you need to be open to it.

We should be cautious with confusing the unfamiliar with the improbable. Just because we didn't expect it doesn't mean that it can't happen. A scenario that we have not yet considered might look strange, but should not be summarily dismissed. A reaction of *"Wow, I never saw that coming. I never looked at it that way before,"* is much more valuable than *"See, I knew it all along. I was right!"* You've learned a lot more in the first of these two scenarios.

Sir John Harvey Jones said:

> Planning is an unnatural process—it's much more fun to get on with it. The real benefit of not planning is that failure comes as a complete surprise and is not preceded by months of worry.

The unfortunate reality with Analytics is that planning is a real necessity. The data might tell a story all by itself, but the story might well be a fairytale if the planning is not rigorous. The knowledge of the experts must be used to inform the Diagnostic Analytics at the outset. With a little ingenuity and a sound foundation of Diagnostics, the Predictive Analytics task can pretty much take care of itself. The humans must once more be involved in setting the direction for the Prescriptive Analytics.

Analytics may be the pathfinder, but the human still needs to hold the compass.

CHAPTER 7

WHERE TO NEXT?

As I conducted my research for this book, I was struck by the divergence of thought that I found in other opinions. The AI debate, not unlike other major scientific developments, brings out polarized positions. Where extreme views were present, they were in evidence with philosophers taking a stance on one side—*"We don't even understand what consciousness is in humans, so thinking that we can bring that capability to machines is absurd"*—and mathematicians or computer scientists arguing without equivocation on the other side. Others were truly frightened that, ungoverned, the developments in AI would, to echo Elon Musk, become *"our greatest existential threat."* In terms of a common vision of the future, not much has changed since the Minsky / Englebart debate in the 1960s that I referenced in **Chapter 2**.

> MINSKY: We're going to make machines intelligent. We are going to make them conscious!
>
> ENGELBART: You're going to do all that for the machines? What are you going to do for the people?

But while polarized positions still exist, there is enough evidence of advancement in AI, of its impact on our lives, and on the lives of others, that there is a strategic imperative to respond. This, I feel, is no longer a matter of opinion.

What Do We Know?

As one of my college professors used to say: *"We are all entitled to our own opinions, but we are not entitled to our own facts"*.

The facts are clear:

1. AI is impacting your personal and professional life today, and the impact will only increase in the short and medium term.
2. AI is replacing jobs at a rate that is materially significant and cannot be ignored. AI is moving from consumer- or task-based utility, to applications that are more knowledge-worker focused — though there are still many application areas that are beyond the capability of the machines.
3. AI is getting smarter. (Most of the time we don't notice.)
4. All AI systems need to be taught about the domain to which they are being applied. This is a critical, but often overlooked, aspect of AI.
5. The harvest from AI systems is dependent on the bias of those who plant the seeds or nourish the crop (see **Chapter 9**).
6. Most of the effective AI systems in use today are dependent on ginormous datasets.
7. Big Data works when you truly have Big Data, but only when you know the big questions. Small Data matters

too and that fact is particularly relevant to knowledge workers today.

8. (AI + Humans) is greater than the sum of the parts. Knowledge remains a core differentiator for knowledge workers.

In a BBC account, from August 2016, entitled *Foxconn replaces 60,000 factory workers with robots,* it was reported that Foxconn Technology Group, the Chinese manufacturing company that is a major supplier to Apple and Samsung, was replacing 60,000 employees with robots. According to Foxconn:

> We are applying robotics engineering and other innovative manufacturing technologies to replace repetitive tasks previously done by employees, and through training, also enable our employees to focus on higher value-added elements in the manufacturing process, such as research and development, process control and quality control.

This quote from Foxconn captures the essence of the current state of AI in two important dimensions. The first dimension to consider is that AI is being applied effectively in lower-value repetitive tasks. It is perhaps a cruel irony that it is low-cost economies that are most at risk from the advancements in AI in the short-term. Jobs were first outsourced from the more expensive countries that placed more value on knowledge-based activities. Now, many of the tasks that were outsourced to cheap workers will next be outsourced to the cloud. This is simply an extension of the use of technology to increase efficiencies, and is merely an evolution of the trend that we have seen for decades. AI will enable automation to address more tasks than before, and it will continue to progress up the knowledge curve. We all need to be prepared for how this will impact our work and our companies.

While Foxconn is reportedly replacing workers at the lower end of the value curve, its stated goal of up-skilling its workers to contribute *"higher value-added elements"* demonstrates an awareness of the need to make humans smarter at the same time as we are infusing machines with intelligence. This is the second dimension and is one that we must all consider now. **Humans need to be enabled and augmented to carry out more value-add roles.**

The Paris-headquartered consulting firm, Capgemini, announced, also in August 2016, that it has replaced 30% to 40% of the work done by its resource management group with IBM's cognitive computing system, Watson. The company is looking at ways to drive more efficiency in its HR system. *"If in the past we had to look at 100 resumes to hire one person, we are looking at how that can be brought to 20, so that we can better target whom we are picking. We are also putting some part of the assessment—like tests—online, so that less time can be spent interviewing candidates,"* said Ashwin Yardi of Capgemini. This is a real live example of AI progress up the knowledge curve. **AI is being applied to tasks today that traditionally would have been the preserve of the knowledge worker.**

IBM's Watson helped Hollywood's biggest film production house, 20th Century Fox, to come up with a trailer for its new fictional suspense movie *Morgan*. Fox approached IBM and asked if Watson could analyze the movie and generate a trailer automatically. Watson analyzed over 100 horror / thriller movie trailers and their individual scenes to understand the components of sound, speech, music, picture, scene, and emotion and extracted the 10 best candidate moments from the entire *Morgan* movie that could be used for the trailer, which an IBM filmmaker edited and arranged in a clip format. *"Watson is a tool that understands visuals but still needs human element to supervise the creative elements,"* commented Zef Cota, filmmaker at IBM Research.

Even though Watson's ability to process the entire *Morgan* movie and to suggest trailer moments is incredibly impressive from a technology perspective, it had to be taught using training data from the 100 other movie trailers before it could begin its task and it needed the 'human element' for the creative task. **AI is getting smarter, but the machine still needs to be taught and it cannot be creative.**

When Apple was subjected to criticism for the poor initial performance of Siri, and users became frustrated with its shortcomings, Apple gave Siri a brain transplant. Deciding that tweaks would not be sufficient to fix the problems, Apple moved Siri voice recognition to a neural-net based system, which now leverages Machine Learning (ML) techniques. Siri still looks the same, but now it is supercharged with deep learning. It can answer some pretty detailed questions—as long as the questions are based on topics that can be easily codified, where the data exists and there is not a requirement for interpretation or judgment.

As you can see from the iPhone screenshots in **Figures 23 and 24**, the queries that Siri can handle are getting more complex. In the first screenshot it is simply converting the words *"Who is the best guitarist in the world?"* to a search term and bringing back the normal search results that you would expect. When asked, *"How do I make apple pie?"* in the second screenshot, Siri found a Wikipedia entry to help. I then asked it to *"Show me a good movie with Tom Hanks"* and it listed 24 Tom Hanks movies ranked by audience rating. It understood what 'good' meant.

Figure 23: SIRI RESPONSES—1

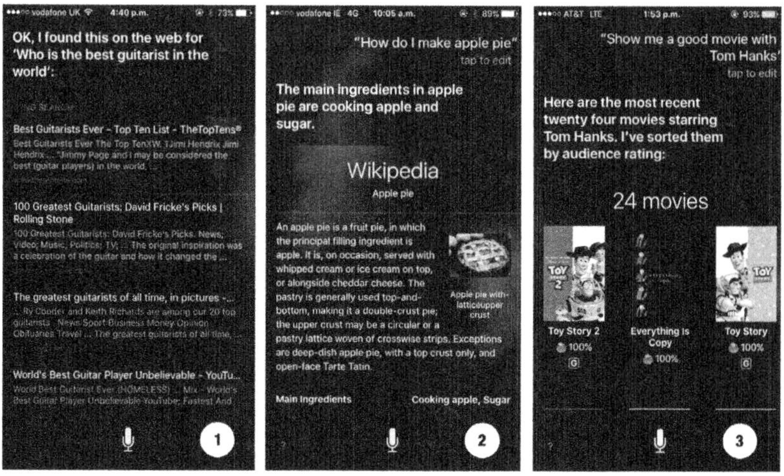

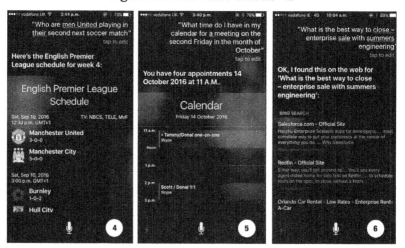

Siri displayed a deeper NLP (Natural Language Processing) capability when the fourth question was *"Who are men (sic) United playing in the second next soccer match?"*

Figure 24: SIRI RESPONSES—2

It figured out what 'second next' meant, and displayed the details. The verbal response from Siri also referred to this game as the 'Manchester Derby' — pretty impressive.

For the fifth question, I tackled a routine business task: *"What time do I have in my calendar for a meeting on the second Friday in the month of October?"* Siri had access to the information in my calendar, it understood what 'the second Friday in the month of October' meant and showed me my calendar for that day — very helpful and a common feature of many of the virtual assistants available today.

Then, in the final question, I asked, *"What is the best way to close the enterprise sale with Summers Engineering?"* Of course, Siri had no clue. It did not have any data, context or knowledge to use. It would have needed access to a system like Altify Max described in **Chapter 4,** where the knowledge is already baked in.

AI systems today are certainly getting smarter, but only when the task to which they are being applied can be reduced to a codified set of signals that they can understand. **For knowledge workers, AI can help with easily defined tasks that can be reduced to binary signals. For all others, the knowledge must be embedded into the system.**

Where Do I Go from Here?

When Salesforce launches its Salesforce Einstein platform at Dreamforce in October 2016, it will be bringing AI capabilities to the knowledge worker. The platform will likely include ML capabilities and limited domain knowledge in the application areas that it already services with its various 'Clouds,' like Sales Cloud, Marketing Cloud and Service Cloud. Other companies that provide cloud-based solutions in the enterprise will surely follow suit, so this is a good time to think about what you should do next.

I will focus my thoughts on those who are active in the knowledge economy—particularly Sales, Marketing, and Customer Service:

1. Embrace the arrival of AI (particularly the Augmented variety) as a positive force for the enablement of knowledge workers.

2. Decide what tasks currently being undertaken by your knowledge workers, such as data collection, data processing, scheduling, reporting, can be offloaded to the machine.

3. Look at your most value-add activities—those that require the application of expertise, such as strategic sales, marketing strategy, and customer engagement – and consider how these activities would be better if augmented with core domain knowledge. Solving this problem will deliver rapid competitive advantage.

4. Before embarking on any Analytics or Big Data project, consider first the questions that you need to answer that will move the needle in your business.

5. Remember that most value-add tasks for knowledge workers are not great candidates for ML or mere data analysis. In most cases the datasets are too small, so ML does not work. Your return will be much greater if you can figure out how to apply knowledge to the small quantify of data that you have to gain insight.

AI is just the next step in automation—though it is a very significant step. The efficacy of any project will be dependent not just on technology or technical feasibility. The costs of the project, the value of the work, the scarcity or otherwise of the skills needed will all need to be considered. In the context of knowledge work, you will get greater return from investing in the humans—augmenting the knowledge worker with Augmented Intelligence—rather than delegating the thinking to the machine. After all, knowledge workers think for a living, and we will benefit by making that thinking more informed.

Final Thoughts

While it is clear that AI in general, and ML particularly, has changed how we interact with technology, it does not necessarily follow that we must ourselves change at the core. The ML mindset is at odds with the human condition of self-determination and we should not abrogate our responsibility to shape our own decisions or future—just because it is easier. We need to control our own user experience, and that of our colleagues and customers, today and tomorrow. When engineers use AI and ML, they cannot step back and let unguided software discover solutions and we should counsel against that. There is still a role for human governance—perhaps it is even more critically needed when we start training a system based on large data sets of human behavior. We must remain the curators of thought, knowledge and human behavior.

Our most distinguishing attributes are our consciousness and intelligence, our capacity for empathy and creativity, free will and moral choices. This is a very exciting time, replete with new possibilities and opportunity, but we must all be the conscious and deliberate authors of our own future. That is true today and it will be just as true tomorrow.

Donal Daly, September 2016

P.S. Thank you for taking the time to read this far. You could stop here; but in the next section, **Inside the Machine**, there are two additional chapters that provide greater insight into what is going on in the guts of the computers and minds of the engineers and programmers who designed them.

SECTION 2

INSIDE THE MACHINE

CHAPTER 8

AN INTRODUCTION TO
MACHINE LEARNING

Chapter 1 suggested that the future of knowledge workers is (probably) secure for now. It is not really as simple as that. It is worthwhile considering this at a more granular level, and reflecting on the different types of undertakings that knowledge workers in business are tasked with. Elements of this work will undoubtedly become the preserve of the machine, and humans, who are more prone to error when completing repetitive tasks, will need to move up the knowledge curve (see **Figure 5**) to sustain the differentiated advantage over the machine and to continue to be relevant.

Nevertheless, I am confident that, in our lifetimes, *appropriately skilled* knowledge workers *who are using the best of the available technology* will remain as the vanguard of strategy, judgment, culture, management, design, and creativity, in so far as, for the particular task or occupation, knowledge and experience differentiate one human's performance from another. For tasks that fall into this general sentient category there are limitations to what the machines can do today, and for the foreseeable future.

Pairing human and machine—the heart of Augmented Intelligence—is the optimum solution for maximizing the effectiveness of tasks that require sentience—the ability to think—but also benefit from a 'fairly' consistent process or methodology to guide the actor. In the business world, consulting best practices, architectural design, sales or procurement methodology, financial audits, legal contract assessment, and employee performance reviews are all examples of activities that cannot be fully automated today with traditional AI or Machine Learning (ML). For the most part, computers cannot yet learn unless they are taught basic knowledge and fed lots of data. That's where Augmented Intelligence comes to the fore. However, it is good to understand ML concepts, opportunities and constraints, so that you can make way for the machine to do its thing and spend your time focused on what you can do.

By the way, you should consider the fact that Google, Facebook, Amazon, etc.—the companies that are driving the future evolution of the Internet—are obsessed with ML. **If nothing else gets your attention, that fact should.** Because these companies have a heavy influence on the future of the Internet, they will have a material impact on our lives—at least for those of us who see the Internet as an important part of the future. Don't ignore Machine Learning.[6]

---

[6]   Disclaimer: This is not intended to be a technology dissertation on Machine Learning. In my wanderings through the concepts over the next few pages, I will err on the side of simplicity – so that I can cover it efficiently – rather than on scientific or engineering accuracy. It's not wrong, but it's not complete either.

A Brief Introduction to Machine Learning

The most pervasive learning, recognition, pattern-matching engine today is the human. We are better at recognizing a bird in a tree than a computer will ever be. If a baby is sitting on its head covered in peanut butter, we still know it is a baby, and we still know which end is the head. When we knock our shins against the edge of a low coffee table, we learn pretty quickly that we should not do that again. We are pretty advanced machines. But we are not perfect, sometimes not predictable, and we are certainly not programmatic or scalable. There are things that we suck at that machines do really well.

ML is a technique that uses algorithms on datasets to help you uncover insight from data. An algorithm is usually derived from a dataset of historical data that describes actual outcomes based on known inputs. To get started on creating the algorithm you need to feed a software program with lots of data that has been organized and tagged by humans. This data is called *training data*. The program can then wander through the data and figure out the algorithm to solve a specific problem. The goal is to make everything programmatic, predictable, and scalable.

Any wiser yet? I didn't think so.

An example might help. If you have read any of my other books you will know I am a bit of a frustrated musician, so I am going to use a music example to explain ML.

Will We Make the Top 10 in the *Billboard* Charts?

Imagine you're an executive working for a record company. You've been around the block, some of your artists have been globally successful and you've been to the parties. Man, the stories you could tell! The industry is in your bones. You just have to listen to the first few bars of a song and you have a good sense of where it will get to on the *Billboard* charts. But now the music industry is changing. It is getting harder to make money without going on tour with the bands. You need someone else to meet all of the new bands and artists and to pick the hit songs.

You decide that it is time to build a ML program that can pick hit songs and estimate where they will end up on *Billboard* charts. As you think about the songs that you have released in the past you list key parameters that you can easily identify and that you think contributed to their position in the charts.

The parameters are:

- **Artist Profile:** When they are hot they are hot.

- **Song Hook:** A killer hook stays in your head and makes the song instantly recognizable. Think Roy Orbison's *Pretty Woman, Dancing Queen* from ABBA, or *Beat It,* one of the seven hit songs from Michael Jackson's *Thriller* album.

- **Song Duration:** Let's face it, *Bohemian Rhapsody* at six minutes is the exception rather than the rule.

- **Genre**: Country is back and hot right now.

You know this data for all of your artists, so you write up a table for the last 100 songs you released—as in **Figure 25**. Critically, you include the highest *Billboard* chart position reached for each song.

Figure 25: PREVIOUS HITS AND THEIR CHART POSITIONS

Song	Artist Profile	Hook	Duration	Genre	Chart #
1	Low	Killer	2:56	Rock	6
2	High	Ok	3:06	Rock	8
3	Stratospheric	Ok	2:48	Country	1
4	Low	Ok	4:16	Alternative	43
5	Low	Killer	3:21	Pop	8
6	High	None	2:36	Country	12
7	Low	Killer	2:57	Country	7
8	High	Ok	3:00	Rock	7
9	Stratospheric	Killer	3:35	Pop	2
10	Low	Ok	5:11	Alternative	56
...					
...					
100	High	Ok	2:85	Rock	9

This is the training data for your ML algorithm—and using it we can create a program to guess where we might end up in the charts for the next new song.

Figure 26: AN ALGORITHM TO PREDICT HIT SONGS

Song	Profile	Hook	Duration	Genre	Chart #
X	High	Killer	2:47	Country	????

This is an example of *Supervised Learning*—just one type of ML. Because we knew the answer—the highest position each song achieved in the charts—we could track backwards through the inputs, to figure out the logic. The more data we can provide, the better chance we have of predicting the *Billboard* chart position.

In Supervised Learning you let the program figure out the relationships and guess at a likely algorithm to arrive at an answer to a prescribed question. There is significant variance in performance of ML in Supervised Learning based on how the humans organize the data AND what attributes we declare as determinant of the outcome. In our example here we could also have included Beat per Minutes, Lyrics and Melody as further elements to consider.

So far we are really just hoping that we picked the right attributes and that they can all be equally applied to work out a likely position in the *Billboard* charts.

The next step is to refine the algorithm by testing its accuracy and then applying weighting factors to each of the attributes that we are using. If we apply the algorithm to another set of songs (say songs 101-200) for which we know the actual results—but that were not part of the training data that we used to build the algorithm, we can see how well we are doing—as in **Figure 27**.

Figure 27: APPLYING THE ALGORITHM

Song	Artist Profile	Hook	Duration	Genre	Algo	Chart #
101	Low	Killer	2:56	Country	4	11
102	High	Ok	3:06	Pop	3	8
103	High	Killer	5:52	Blues	31	67
104	Low	Ok	4:16	Rock	62	13
105	Stratos	Ok	2:52	Country	1	2
...						
...						
200	Stratos	Ok	2:45	Pop	2	1

For songs 105 and 200 we did pretty well—just about as close as we could really ever hope—but the rest of them are a bit of a mess. We need to tweak the algorithm with weighting and /

or extend the dataset to include Beat Per Minutes, Lyrics and Melody as elements to consider.

We may then end up with inputs that look like **Figure 28**.

Figure 28: WEIGHTING THE ELEMENTS OF THE ALGORITHM

Attribute	Weighting
Artist Profile	0.21
Song Hook	0.18
Duration	0.10
Genre	0.05
Beats per Minute	0.08
Lyrics	0.22
Melody	0.16

And when we re-run our test data, we will see that the results are different.

Figure 29: APPLYING THE EXTENDED ALGORITHM

Song	Profile	Hook	Duration	Genre	BPM	Lyrics	Melody	Algo	Chart #
101	Low	Killer	2:56	Country	220	Good	Good	6	11
102	High	Ok	3:06	Pop	240	Killer	Good	11	8
103	High	Killer	5:52	Blues	210	Good	Ok	54	67
104	Low	Ok	4:16	Rock	140	Ok	Good	16	13
105	Stratos	Ok	2:52	Country	222	Killer	Hot	3	2
...									
...									
200	Stratos	Ok	2:45	Pop	212	Killer	Ok	4	1

In some cases, we have improved and in other instances the results have gotten a little worse. For this type of ML to be effective there are approaches that allow you to try many different sets of weightings and combine the outcomes to get an answer that may be closer to the actual results that you want. I have skipped over many steps here, but hope that I have done enough to give you a sense of what people are talking about when they bring up ML.

Correlation and Causation

There is a difference between Correlation and Causation. Songs 105 and 200 are both under 3 minutes long, with killer lyrics. Both got to the top two positions in the charts. However, this does not mean that all songs with those two attributes will achieve that same chart success. Two events can consistently correlate with each other but not have any causal relationship.

For example: If, back in 2008, you were trying to predict the next US President, you might have used training data based on the first 43 presidents. Your predicted outcome would have been not have been a young African-American. The data would have pointed to a different profile altogether. Correlation does not imply causation, but can distract. I discussed this in **Chapter 6**.

Machine Learning for Knowledge Workers in Business

You may not be aware of it but you probably experience ML nearly every day. When you type a search query into Google you will often be prompted with suggestions for your search, and Google will also parse your search query and provide intelligent answers as if your search was completely logical (in the computer sense of logical). Sometimes Google will also suggest answers to questions you have not even asked but that it has learned are likely questions you might want to ask next.

Figure 30: GOOGLE SEARCH RESULTS FOR "HOW OLD IS STEPHEN TYLER?"

Showing results for How old is **steven** tyler
Search instead for How old is stephen tyler

Steven Tyler / Age

68 years

March 26, 1948

Spouse: Teresa Barrick (m. 1988–2006), Cyrinda Foxe (m. 1978–1987)
Height: 5' 10"

 Mick Jagger
73 years

 Liv Tyler
Daughter
39 years

 Axl Rose
54 years

Feedback

People also ask

How old is Steven Tyler 2015?

How many times has Steven Tyler been married?

Is Steven Tyler Italian?

Let's deconstruct the example in **Figure 30**: *"How old is Stephen Tyler?"* For the sake of the example I spelled Steven Tyler's name incorrectly, using 'Stephen' instead of 'Steven.' What happened was:

- Google figured that out, because most people type 'Steven Tyler,' not 'Stephen Tyler.'

- Then Google also decided that if I was interested in knowing his age, then I might be interested in the age of Mick Jagger and Axl Rose also. This suggests to me that this is a common search path.

- Google also figured out that Liv Tyler is Steven Tyler's daughter, so it displayed her age as well, just in case I cared.

- It also prompted me with other questions that 'People also ask.'

There's a lot going on here—Google has a generic ML algorithm that is answering the question: *"When someone types something into the search box, what do they really mean, and what else might they be interested in?"*

Like the other Internet giants, Amazon and Facebook, Google has one very significant advantage over the rest of us. It is dealing with enormous quantities of data. Approximately 3.4 million searches are done every minute on Google. That's about 5 billion searches every day. That's a lot of data to work with. It is not something that you can compare with.

The biggest challenge in applying ML to business is that ML is only as good as the data that you have to work with and, in most cases, the applications that knowledge workers need to solve are *Small Data* problems, not *Big Data* problems. When I say 'Small Data' I mean not colossal Google-scale datasets. In addition to the data problem, the ML software available today is just not good enough for general applications. Some might argue that, if we have enough data, we can work through this but therein lies the problem. You are never going to get enough data. You have to augment it with human intervention. Even the Big Data guys are doing this, and the datasets they are working with are on a scale that most of us can never use.

Figure 31: FACEBOOK PHOTO TAGGING

Facebook is getting better at face recognition because it relies on human intervention to tag photos. It prompts us to tag people in photos and, because you can do it easily and quickly, it is building up massive training data that is used to train its ML models. You will have noticed that Facebook is continuously getting better at suggesting names for your photos. That's ML at work—and we are all part of the solution, helping Facebook to teach its ML models better ways to recognize people's faces. As referenced earlier, Google Search gets better as more people use it and it learns from your searches to provide even better answers to others. Because 'pure' ML is so hard, even the Internet giants are dependent on humans to help their ML models get smarter.

This model of application is referred to as a Reciprocal Data Application (RDA), where applications are designed to encourage users to help teach the ML system by adding informed data to the system through human intervention. RDAs are another example of Augmented Intelligence, in this case applied to applications that have access to *ginormous* datasets. You get the best of both worlds in a blended approach that leverages large amounts of training data, as well as human decision-making expertise alongside powerful computing abilities.

Much of the actual processing, however, is not happening on the computer. In the first instance, the human is doing the thinking, and conceptualizing to create the model. When the model is up and running, comparing new data to the model is computationally cheap. However, making the model smarter requires both knowledge and experience. Humans have an inherent contextual awareness that the computer does not possess unless it has been programmed that way, and humans also have a foundation of experience to apply to the assessment of new data.

The only way to build a useful ML application for knowledge workers, where the datasets are small (and they are always small), is to select a very specialized domain area and then to adopt an approach that borrows heavily from the RDA approach, but takes it to a higher level of human intervention.

What Machine Learning Means for Business

We know that the Internet giants like Facebook, Amazon and Google have a massive advantage when it comes to ML, and they will continue to extend and deepen their advantage in the market because of their existing and growing scale. Since they have lots of users, who spend a lot of time on their sites, and almost limitless ability to invest, it would be pointless to try to compete with them. The good news is that they don't generally (yet) compete in application areas for knowledge workers.

For those of us who are focused on providing or using applications that support knowledge workers, the opportunity is to leverage technologies like ML but to do so with an approach that heavily supports the technology with human-infused knowledge to augment the intelligence in the software. Operating in particular business niches, as opposed to consumer domains, we can differentiate through applications that use unique training data specific to those niches, and enable business knowledge experts to pour their knowledge into the application. This approach compensates for the absence of vast quantities of training data and enables much more accurate outcomes for knowledge-intensive applications.

One application area where this approach can be readily applied is in B2B enterprise sales, where an individual salesperson is responsible for selling reasonably high value products or solutions to large companies. Because B2B sales people typically work less than 100 sales opportunities in a year, the dataset to be mined is very small. Some software companies that provide solutions in this domain have already aggregated data from multiple sales organizations, but the resultant datasets are still tiny in comparison to the large datasets needed for effective ML. However, as with most occupations that require a level of strategy, judgment, management, or creativity, there are already proven structured processes or methodologies that evidentially can guide the protagonist to a high level of success. Rather than focus on the ML capabilities as the core engine to be enhanced by knowledge, applications that serve these knowledge workers are better designed by flipping that approach on its head.

Start with infusing the application with experiential knowledge, and then use 'results-data' to refine the knowledge for the specific context in which the application is being applied. At the core, B2B Sales is similar across all industries. Among other things, the seller must understand the customer's business, the decision criteria being used by the customer to select a vendor, how their product can be used to meet the customer's need, the competitors they are likely to encounter in a deal, and the unique capabilities of their own product. However, there are subtleties that vary from industry to industry. Buyers in healthcare, financial services and pharmaceutical industries will likely be subject to different regulatory constraints than those in manufacturing or technology, and the selling approach, and the smart software that guides them, must be cognizant of that context.

Where it is practical, you will also want to make RDA-like extensions available so that the application can learn from the users in the community where it is applied. Effectively, you are crowd-sourcing knowledge, in a manner similar to Facebook or Google, but just on a much smaller scale. Instead of asking the machine to learn automatically and to adjust its algorithms in real-time, something that is only valid when working with colossal amounts of data, you are using the crowd-source approach to help the application designer or implementer to augment the knowledge that the system is using to create more valuable results for the knowledge worker who is using the application.

While there is an increasing amount of information that knowledge workers have to process, it seems to make sense that where appropriate—and only where appropriate—companies should look to elements of ML, or learn from the approach, to automate delivery of intelligence when possible. More importantly, though, they must build or use applications that allow for augmentation of the intelligence where necessary. This will be one of the most powerful frontiers of competitive advantage through the balance of this decade.

CHAPTER 9

ALGORITHMIC BIAS
– KEEPING HUMANS IN THE LOOP

Bias Is a Natural Human Condition

We are all biased. We habitually see things from our own perspective. We're focused on protecting our own interests. There's a Croatian proverb that goes: *"The hunchback sees the hump of others—never his own."* I think we have all been guilty of that. I know I have. We all have bias that we bring to conversations and everyday situations. We don't often see the other side as clearly as we see our own. But what happens when this bias makes its way into the algorithms that power AI? Bias at scale. We need to be careful.

According to American computer scientist Alan Kay, perspective is worth 80 IQ points. That's worth thinking about. What's the other person's perspective? If we don't know that, then it is hard to make fair assessments or unpartisan decisions. It can result in extreme unintended consequences when prejudice, partiality, bigotry, intolerance, or stereotyping creeps inside the machine and the only limit to the reach of its partisanship is the capacity of the processor.

It is hard to argue with the concept that the design of an algorithm or an AI model reflects the thought processes and ideas of the designer. In **Chapter 8**, when attempting to predict whether a song would be a hit, I arbitrarily selected what I considered might be the factors that might portend its 'hit-ness'—that is, where it would end up on the *Billboard* charts. The attributes I included in my hypothetical Machine Learning model were Artist Profile, Song Hook, Duration, Genre, Beats per Minute, Lyrics, and Melody. This may well be a reasonable list, but it tends towards assessing songs based on my experiences, and as I was thinking though this list I was imagining the bands that I grew up with, the different songs that combined to create the soundtrack of my children's early lives, and the tunes that I have been introduced to by friends and colleagues that I encounter in my travels. My view, and what I viewed as important, could be catalogued as 'middle-aged, mid-Atlantic.' The Machine Learning algorithm that I was notionally building reflected my experiences, included what I know and am familiar with, and ignored that of which I am ignorant. My model is biased.

Here's the conundrum. It is hard to think about any business application that would not be improved by adding a spoonful of automation, a sprinkling of AI, or a *soupçon* of ML. However, it is not difficult to see that the models we build will contain bias as a default condition. We are only human, flawed by nature and honed by nurture.

Most people are fundamentally good, not evil—and this is equally true of creators of algorithms or AI systems. Very few of us wake up in the morning wondering how we can inflict harm or do evil. Most of us want to 'do the right thing.' However, our environment heavily influences each of us and we can never have the whole picture, a complete 360-degree view. Engineers and scientists, researchers and academics strive to create AI systems that will improve some element of society. But 'true north' from a humanistic or morality perspective is directed by every individual's own moral compass and focused or blurred by the breadth or narrowness of one's perspective. The societal noise in the soundtrack of our lives creates bias, or reinforces prejudice, and it would be naïve to think that we can easily block out that noise when we are creating algorithms.

We are shaped by where we were born, what we read, what we experience, and the expressions of our role models. If a lack of understanding is embedded in AI, the digital tapestry becomes pixelated with discord and someone suffers. More often than not, it's worth taking the time to try to get the picture as others have painted it. When machines are endowed with the ability to mass-produce facsimile images, those who are responsible for the creation of the algorithms must recognize the social and moral responsibility that comes with creation of AI or similar systems. We tend to look at computers as objective inanimate objects that do not have opinions or exhibit subjective behavior. But when software programs that are used to take decisions, shape opinion, or make recommendations inherit the proclivities of their creators, then subjectivity will inevitably surface, and will likely do so at Internet speed.

There are already too many examples of algorithms infected with bias:

- Google is more likely to advertise executive-level salaried positions to search engine users if it thinks the user is male, according to a Carnegie Mellon study.[7]

---

[7] http://www.andrew.cmu.edu/user/danupam/dtd-pets15.pdf.

- Harvard researchers found that ads about arrest records were much more likely to appear alongside searches for names thought to belong to a black person *versus* a white person.[8]

It doesn't stop at the original algorithm or model. If the architect of a ML program managed to build a completely unbiased model, but furnishes the program with the ability to learn from data, he or she still needs to be aware of the possibility of bias seeping into the process. When the dataset is informed by human interaction, and the model learns from that interaction, the designers need to add some guardrails or monitoring services into the system.

The smarter we make our machines, the more diverse we need to make the creators, so that the product of their creations doesn't discriminate. Innovators tend to innovate first and clean up any mess that has been created by the innovation afterwards. It is not always safety first. In the case of AI, however, I would hope that there might just be sufficient awareness of the massive potential for good or evil and that maybe greater care will be taken.

AI can actually provide us with an opportunity to reduce discrimination, or to achieve more balanced perspective at scale. First, we need to recognize that AI has the potential to cause harm and that algorithms can be wrong and they can be amoral. Sometimes that may be because of how they have been designed. On other occasions, if they have been equipped with self-adjusting algorithms, machines can learn to be biased or amoral through their interaction with humans. We should constantly reflect on the general human condition and we must take care.

---

[8]   http://dataprivacylab.org/projects/onlineads/1071-1.pdf.

Google Reflects the Bias in Human Behavior

When the Google search engine returns its search results, it gives you two types: organic and paid. Even though paid results are given prominent placement, organic search results are 8.5x more likely to be clicked on than paid search results. Users know the difference and recognize that organic results are typically the more respected source.

Figure 32: GOOGLE SEARCH RESULTS: PAID AND ORGANICS

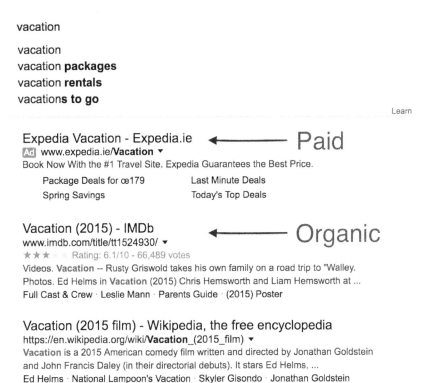

The search results are influenced by a number of factors. In the case of paid search, the bias is pretty clear. Generally speaking, as an advertiser, the more money you pay to

Google for certain 'keywords,' the more likely it is that your link or your ad will appear.

Organic search results are based on a number of personalization factors—for example, Google will attempt to prioritize results that are closer to your location—but primarily the results you see are driven by the behaviors of others on the web.

You will have noticed that, as you start to enter your search term into Google, it predicts the question that you are really asking. This can result in a view into popular opinion that can be disturbing, reflecting the bias of millions of users. Typing *"women shouldn't have"* into the Google search box highlights a body of opinion that questions whether women should have rights.

Figure 33: GOOGLE SEARCH RESULTS FOR "WOMEN SHOULDN'T HAVE"

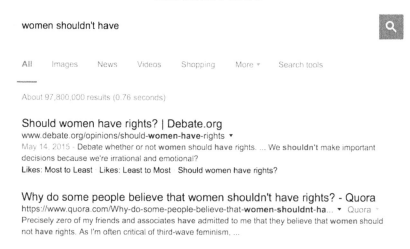

A similar search, this time for *"men shouldn't have"* results showed much more benign behavior.

Figure 34: GOOGLE SEARCH RESULTS FOR "MEN SHOULDN'T HAVE"

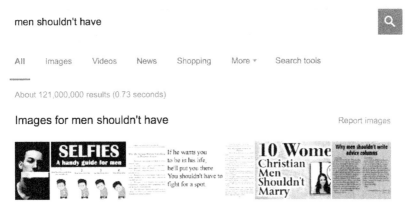

men shouldn't have

All   Images   Videos   News   Shopping   More ▾   Search tools

About 121,000,000 results (0.73 seconds)

Images for men shouldn't have   Report images

More images for men shouldn't have

Things Men Shouldn't Do After 30 - AskMen
www.askmen.com/top_10/dating/things-**men-shouldnt**-do-after-30.html ▾ AskMen ▾
Apr 2, 2016 - Nope, not cool to stereotype like that even if it was. It was written by a man. To me, there's a lot of truth to this, though it has a judgemental tone.

This Is Only for Women, Men Shouldn't Read - Kevin A. Thompson
www.kevinathompson.com/this-is-only-for-wo**men-men-shouldnt**-read/ ▾
This Is Only for Women, **Men Shouldn't** Read. Apr 042013 Kevin A. Thompson ... Because I'm a guy, I've never had the guts to say it. Until now... Proverbs 7 tells ...

Men Shouldn't Wear Flip-Flops, But Not Because Feet Are Gross
www.huffingtonpost.com/.../should-**men**-wear-flip-flops_us_577... ▾ The Huffington Post ▾
Men Shouldn't Wear Flip-Flops, But Not Because Feet Are Gross. This debate has no sole. 07/05/2016 05:15 pm ET. 1.8k. James Cave Men's Lifestyle Editor, ...

Google Search is the most widely used ML algorithmically-driven application in the world. It reflects our thoughts and exposes our curiosity and the topics about which we are curious. The human condition is complex and none of us fully understands the perspectives or motivations of others. That is evident when we look at the way Google search responds. When ML is informed by human behavior, the designers of the underlying software programs have a responsibility to build in corrective systems to weed out bias as soon as it creeps into the system.

Bias in the Algorithm

Sometimes, though, the bias is built into the algorithm. In 2015, pediatrician Dr. Louise Selby found that she could not use her security passcode to enter the female changing rooms at a gym in Cambridge, England, because the algorithm that was powering the security system had been programmed to think that anyone who was a doctor had to be male.

The Dr. Selby story is an example of where the algorithm is sexist. You might argue that someone just made a mistake, or didn't think it through, but such unthinking behavior perpetuates stereotypes and reflects a diversity gap that is all too pervasive in technology companies.

Founders Larry Page and Sergey Brin adopted *"Don't be evil"* as Google's original company motto. (It was replaced in 2015 with *"Do the right thing"*). Whether you believe that Page and Brin were sincere when they first unveiled *"Don't be evil"* there is a significant need to reaffirm similar values today in the age of AI. Google has a gap to overcome when it comes to diversity. According to a report in *USA Today* in July 2015, seven out of 10 Google employees are men. Most employees are white (60%) and Asian (31%). Latinos made up just 3% of the work force and African Americans just 2% — a far cry from the company reflecting the racial and ethnic diversity of its users in the USA and around the world.

Facebook has also become embroiled in algorithmic bias allegations and was subject to a Senate inquiry over claims of anti-conservative bias in its Trending Topics section. Facebook subsequently announced changes to the way it runs its Trending Topics feed. Whether Facebook is anti-conservative or not, what was not considered by many is the fact that Facebook is at heart a commercial organization, and the stories that it wants shown are those that maximize click-ability. It has a profound bias to surface stories that will cause its users to engage and that bias is likely to override any desire it has to influence its political leanings. This is an understandable commercial bias, but one that is not particularly transparent.

In May 2016, ProPublica published a damning article on the use of algorithms in the criminal justice system. According to its website, ProPublica is an independent, non-profit newsroom that produces investigative journalism in the public interest. The article, called *Machine Bias*, concerns the use of algorithms in the judicial sentencing process. It suggests that there are inherent racial biases in the algorithms and that the algorithmic system underestimates the likelihood that white criminals will commit crime again in the future, while overestimating the recidivism of black criminals. Recidivism—a criminal's propensity to commit a future crime—is a major factor in determining prison sentences and rehabilitation requirements, so it is an important factor to get right in the algorithm.

The algorithm in question is called Compas (Correctional Offender Management Profiling for Alternative Sanctions). When defendants are booked into jail, they respond to a Compas questionnaire and their answers are fed into the software to generate predictions of "risk of recidivism" and "risk of violent recidivism." According to the ProPublica analysis of Compas, black defendants who did not reoffend over a two-year period were nearly twice as likely to have been misclassified as 'higher risk' compared with their white counterparts; white defendants who reoffended within the next two years had been mistakenly labeled as 'low risk' almost twice as often as black reoffenders. In its report ProPublica cites two examples and questions why the white criminal received a much lower risk rating than the black criminal.

Figure 35: **PROPUBLICA RECIDIVISM EXAMPLES**

Name	Prior Offences	Subsequent Offenses	Color	Risk
V.P.	2 armed robberies, 1 attempted armed robbery	1 grand theft	White	3
B.B.	4 juvenile misdemeanors	None	Black	8

The prediction of recidivism was influenced by the answers to a 137-question questionnaire, including questions like:

- *#32 If you lived with both parents and they were later separated, how old were you at the time?*

- *#39: How many of your friends / acquaintances have ever been arrested?*

- *#43: Have you ever been a gang member?*

As you might expect there was a lot of reaction to the ProPublica report. Some commentators were outraged at the notion that a machine might have sway over sentencing in the criminal system. Others make the argument that at least the computer is not going to practice nepotism or be influenced by relationships between judge and the defendants' lawyers, suggesting that any racial bias in the algorithm is not as dangerous as the mercurial nature of human racial bias.

Are We Biased Against Algorithms?

I don't profess to have enough knowledge of the criminal justice system domain to express an informed opinion as to the efficacy or fairness of the underlying algorithm in this case reported by ProPublica. However, it seems to me that a well-versed lawyer may be able to coach a defendant on how to answer the questions to get a lighter risk rating and the weightings of the questions themselves in the creation of the algorithm are very open to subjectivity. **The bigger question, though, is not whether the algorithm itself is biased, but whether it is less biased than the human approach.**

This in itself highlights a bias against algorithms, as algorithms are held to a higher standard than humans. Algorithms suffer from the fact that they actually quantify their predictions and can be evaluated after the prediction event more so than *ad hoc* predictions made by humans. But even if algorithms are better at making decisions than humans, once we have seen them fail we are less inclined to use them again. This is anti-algorithm bias. In contrast, if we see humans fail in their decision-making processes we are more likely to rationalize their shortcomings. This is pro-human bias.

If it turns out that algorithms are actually less biased than humans, then avoiding them has the potential to increase, or at least perpetuate, societal bias. Because *ex ante* algorithmic data is available, unlike human bias, the assessment of which is less scientific and subject to opinion and bias itself, we can be definitively aware of algorithmic bias. This is surely a good thing—not the bias itself obviously, but the ability to measure the bias in an algorithm. Once weaknesses have been identified in an algorithm there is an opportunity to adjust and refine. The question then is to determine how to minimize algorithmic prejudice in the first place, and then have a mechanism to measure any bias that exists.

Putting Humans in the Loop

There has long existed a concept that automated systems benefit from having a Human-in-the-Loop (HITL) (**Figure 36**) that allows the user to change the outcome of an event or process. In HITL systems, a human operator is a crucial component of a control system—being the final arbiter of the outcome.

Figure 36: HUMAN-IN-THE-LOOP SYSTEMS

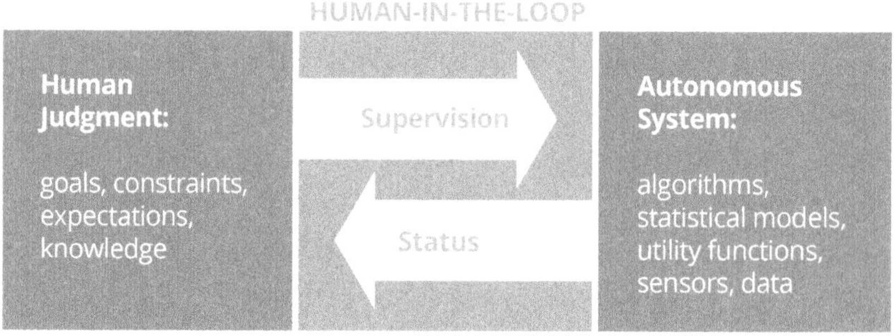

HUMAN-IN-THE-LOOP

Human Judgment:

goals, constraints, expectations, knowledge

Supervision

Status

Autonomous System:

algorithms, statistical models, utility functions, sensors, data

Iyad Rahwan, Associate Professor at the Massachusetts Institute of Technology (MIT) has coined a term *Society-in-the-Loop* (SITL) (**Figure 37**), to describe an extension of the HITL principle, proposing that as more and more governance functions get encoded into AI algorithms, we need to create channels between human values and governance algorithms.

Rahwan suggests that to close the loop, we also need new metrics and methods to evaluate AI behavior against quantifiable human values. He advocates for new tools to enable society to *program, debug, and monitor the algorithmic social contract* between humans and governance algorithms.

Figure 37: **SOCIETY-IN-THE-LOOP SYSTEMS**

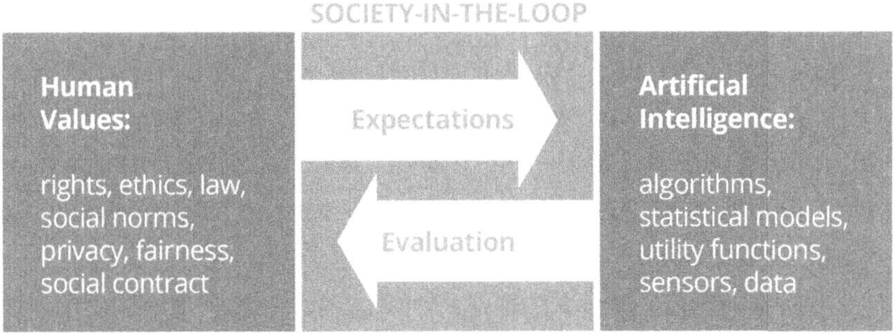

SOCIETY-IN-THE-LOOP

Human Values:	Expectations →	Artificial Intelligence:
rights, ethics, law, social norms, privacy, fairness, social contract	← Evaluation	algorithms, statistical models, utility functions, sensors, data

As reported in *Forbes* in July 2016, a team of researchers at Boston University and Microsoft Research showed how once an algorithm's biases have been quantified, its mathematical properties can be adjusted to model those biases out of its results. The researchers used a large dataset of news content to see how words would fit into the linguistic landscape. Using this dataset one can extract relationships from the data such as: "*man is to king as woman is to queen.*" However, the Boston and Microsoft researchers discovered in their new research that the relationships encoded in this data are heavily gender-biased, reflecting the simple sad fact that news content tends to encode the gender biases of the societies it reflects and the reporters that produce it. For example, the relationship "*man is to computer programmer*" yields as its female equivalent in the dataset "*woman is to homemaker.*"

Here, the researchers found that, by using spot human reviews of the relationships, they could construct a mathematical model of the dataset's gender bias and then essentially create a mirror image of this bias that is then combined with the original data to negate the effect of the bias. In short, the researchers were able to identify and then remove the bias from the data, creating a new non-gender-biased dataset.

The solution was the use of human reviewers on Amazon Mechanical Turk[9] to review the linguistic relationships in the dataset and to flag the ones they viewed as gender-biased. The final model is therefore not truly unbiased but rather combines the biases in the original dataset with the biases of the Mechanical Turkers, to create a kind of antidote to the algorithmic bias.

The SITL principles—important in the broader conversation about the societal impact of AI, to address some of the concerns of Stephen Hawking, Elon Musk and Bill Gates that I referenced in **Chapter 1**—also have a parallel implementation in the application of AI for knowledge workers. In the work that we do at Altify, the first governing principle that we apply to the Augmented Intelligence solutions that we build is: *First, better to not provide any advice at all than to provide the wrong advice.* In the same way that we hold algorithms to a higher standard of accuracy, we also tend to act on the pronouncements of algorithms more readily than we do the advice of humans. When was the last time you questioned the directions given to you by the navigation system in your car, or by Google Maps?

If we apply the SITL axiom to AI for knowledge workers, we recognize that bias exists in all AI systems—the only difference being the scale of the impact of the bias. It suggests that we can't just let the machine learn from data patterns or unguided analytics and that the signals we identify as the predictors of outcomes are the foundation on which an

---

[9]   Amazon Mechanical Turk provides a service where businesses can utilize crowdsourcing through the Amazon network to use many humans to carry out tasks that are difficult for machines to undertake. Examples of such tasks include transcribing audio files, proofreading documents or assessing the quality of data.

effective system is built. The SITL axiom also demands that those who are the creators of AI tools for domain-specific applications build or use tools that provide for effective knowledge acquisition and representation by the domain experts—those who have the knowledge being modeled in the system—and not just the engineers and scientists who are skilled in building the models. Then we need a closed loop system where those who use the system—the target users that we endeavor to up-skill with the application—can provide feedback on the accuracy and efficacy of the output. That way any inherent bias or sub-optimal knowledge encapsulation can be captured and improved.

Looking to the Future

Is there a need for governance or regulation? The *Sarbanes Oxley Act* was passed by the US Congress in 2002: its purpose was to protect shareholders and the general public from accounting errors and fraudulent practices in enterprises, as well as to improve the accuracy of corporate disclosures. I am generally a proponent of less regulation, but I wonder whether some standards or advisory structure might be valuable or necessary in the future as algorithmic decision-making systems propagate.

The fear of failure is a very powerful motivator, and the apocalyptic headlines of machines corrupting humanity and ruining our lives can evoke visions that suggest failure at speed and scale. But if history teaches us anything, it demonstrates that the human race doesn't need algorithmic assistance to fail at scale—the Somme, the Holocaust and Hiroshima / Nagasaki were not our finest moments—and we should look to an AI-enabled future with measured optimism.

Perhaps these powerful new tools can help us better understand and reduce bias. We have never had the tools to do that before. Maybe machines will help humans become better people.

An increasing number of researchers from both the humanities and computer science have recognized the SITL gap, and are making concerted efforts to bridge it. These include novel methods for quantifying algorithmic discrimination, approaches to quantify bias in news filtering algorithms, surveys that elicit the public's moral expectations from machines, means for specifying acceptable privacy-utility tradeoffs, and so on. As algorithms learn bias from their training data, their mathematical purity and transparent underpinnings allow us to peer inside them and understand what they've learned from the data that is fed to them by humans.

We need to augment the behavior of machines at every step in the process. In those areas where data is not available in gigantic quantities we need to understand that erroneous correlations and mistaken predictions are likely and human intervention is more important. In every case we should recognize that, from small seeds, mighty oaks grow. We must be sure we are planting the right seeds in the machine that we can nurture for a more inclusive and respectful world.

INDEX

1-Click®, 8
20th Century Fox, *Morgan*, 122-123
451 Research, 95, 96-97
ABBA, *Dancing Queen*, 133
AGI, *see* Artificial General
    Intelligence
aging workforce, 48-51
AI, *see* Artificial Intelligence
Airbus A380, 11
algorithm(s), 27, 45, 52-53, 132-137,
    143, 145-160
    bias against, 154-155
    intelligent, 39, 40
    judicial sentencing, 153-154
    news filtering, 160
algorithmic
    bias, *see* bias, algorithmic
    discrimination, *see*
    discrimination, algorithmic
Alphabet (formerly Google), *see*
    also Google, 76
Altify, 79-89, 158
Altify Max, 79-89, 125
    Augmented Intelligence
    Insight Engine, 88

Insight Editor, 83, 84, 86
Insight Signal(s), 83, 84, 85, 86,
    89
Insight(s), 84, 85, 86, 88, 89
    Notification(s), 86
Amazon, 76, 93-94, 131, 139
    Mechanical Turk, 158
An Astonishing Record—of Complete
    Failure, 105
Analytics, 20, 90-103, 104-118
    Augmented, 104-118
    bias-free, *see* bias-free analytics
    Descriptive, *see* Descriptive
    Analytics
    Diagnostic, *see* Diagnostic
    Analytics
    four stages of, 107-111
    Predictive, *see* Predictive
    Analytics
    Prescriptive, *see* Prescriptive
    Analytics
Analytics Trends 2016—The Next
    Evolution, 90
Angkor Wat UNESCO world
    heritage site, Cambodia, 66

anti-algorithm bias, *see* bias, anti-
    algorithm
Apple, 9, 61, 76, 121, 123
    Car, 62
    iPhone, 67, 123-124
    Siri, 9, 30, 62, 123-125
application domain, 61, 91, 158
Artificial General Intelligence, 30
Artificial Intelligence, 4, 9-10, 15,
    17, 18, 19, 21, 24-40, 39, 43, 47,
    50-53, 59-60, 62, 70, 71, 76, 77,
    78, 80, 81, 89, 90, 91, 92, 119-
    127, 131, 145-160
    facts, 120-121
    governance / regulation, 159
    model, 146
    polarized opinions, 26, 119-120
    strong, 30
    weak / narrow, 30-32, 36, 62
Asimov, Isaac, *Three Laws of
    Robots*, 25
ATD, 80
Audi, 58
Augmented Intelligence, 4, 9-10,
    15, 17, 20, 35, 40, 41-53, 59-60,
    64-69, 70-89, 90, 91, 126, 127,
    131, 141, 158
    components of application, 66-
    69, 81-86
Augmented Reality, 12
automation, 37, 38, 47, 126
autonomous car(s), *see* car(s),
    autonomous
autonomous driving system(s), 62
Autor, David
    Polanyi's Paradox, 42

*Why Are There Still So Many
    Jobs? The History and Future of
    Workplace Automation*, 47-48
Baby Boomer(s), 50
Back to the Future, 104
BBC, *Foxconn replaces 60,000 factory
    workers with robots*, 121
Beat It, 133
Beck, Jeff, *The Loud Hailer*, 92
Benioff, Marc, 71, 74, 75, 78
BeyondCore, 77
bias, 21, 120, 145-160
    algorithmic, 145-160
    anti-algorithm, 155
Big Data, 4, 8, 15, 18, 20, 81, 90-103,
    112, 120
    attributes, 99-100
    market forecasts, 94
Big Data Analytics, 77, 95, 99, 112
Big Five technology companies, 1,
    4, 6, 7
Billboard charts, 132-137, 146
BMW, 58
Bohemian Rhapsody, 133
Boston University, 157
Brin, Sergey, 152
Brynjolfsson, Erik, *The Second
    Machine Age*, 46-47
Business Analytics, 94-98
Business Intelligence, 94-95, 108
    market forecasts, 97

CAGR, *see* compound annual
    growth rate
Capgemini, 122
car(s)
    autonomous, 53, 57-59
    driverless, 20, 63

self-driving, 40, 54, 59
self-parking, 30
Carnegie Mellon University, 62-63, 147
causation *versus* correlation, 109-110, 137
CBS Interactive, 98
CEB, 80
Chernobyl, 28
Chomsky, Noam, 2
cloud computing, 10, 71, 74
CMU, *see* Carnegie Mellon University
Compas, 153-154
competitive advantage, 18, 72, 89, 99, 126, 144
compound annual growth rate, 96-97
confounding variable, 110
Congress (US), 159
Consensus Forecasts, 105
Coolan, 77
correlation *versus* causation, 109-110, 137
Cortana, 9
Cota, Zef, 123
Crady, Mark, 65
Cramton, Steven, 44
creativity, 20, 45, 61, 127, 130, 142
CRM, *see* Customer Relationship Management
crowd-sourcing, 143
Crunchbase, 75, 77
Customer Relationship Management, 75, 78, 83, 85, 97, 108
    market forecasts, 97
Cyc, 9, 10

Daly, Donal, *Expert Systems Introduced*, 9
Dancing Queen, 133
Darwin, Charles, 33
dataset(s), 21, 48, 53, 97, 103, 120, 126, 132, 136, 139, 141, 142, 148, 157-158
decision-making, 37, 87, 102, 141, 155, 159
Deep Blue, *see* IBM, Deep Blue
Deloitte, *Analytics Trends 2016— The Next Evolution*, 90-91
DeLorean, 104
Descriptive Analytics, 4, 77, 103, 108-109
Diageo, 5
Diagnostic Analytics, 77, 103, 108-109, 118
discrimination, algorithmic, 160
Disney World, 5-6
Dobrov, Vladimir, 44
domain expert(s), 68, 84, 88, 89, 158
domain(-specific) knowledge / expertise, 8, 16, 37, 48, 53, 78, 79, 82, 89, 105, 106, 112, 114, 125, 126
Dominguez, Frank, 74
Downtime, 114
Dreamforce, 71, 125
driverless car(s), *see* car(s), driverless
Dropbox, 93
Drucker, Peter, 71-73
EasyMile, 57-58
eHarmony, 5
Einstein, Albert, 16
eLearning, 80

Eliot, T.S., 3
Englebart, Doug, 52, 119
enterprise software, market
    forecasts, 98
ERP, market forecasts, 97
Excel, 99
experience, 3, 5, 9, 17, 18, 31, 37, 49,
    50, 51, 61, 71, 105, 107, 113, 114,
    117, 130, 141, 146
expert system, definition, 10
Expert Systems Introduced, 9, 10
expertise, 36, 37, 87, 114, 126, 141
Facebook, 76, 88, 131, 139, 143
    algorithmic bias allegations,
    152-153
    photo tagging, 140
Fagen, Donald
    The Nightfly, 92
fax, 93
fear of missing out, 2
FedEx, 94
feedback, 116, 159
Firstmark Capital, 98
Fitness First, 6
Flikr, 93
FOMO, *see* fear of missing out
Forbes, 157
    *Roundup of Analytics, Big Data
    & BI Forecasts and Market
    Estimates, 2016*, 94
foresight, 104-105, 107
Forrester Research, *The Death of the
    B2B Salesman*, 34-35
Forrester Sales Enablement
    Forum, 35
Fortune, 72
Fourth Industrial Revolution, 27-
    28

*Foxconn replaces 60,000 factory
    workers with robots*, 121
Foxconn Technology Group, 121,
    122
Fukushima, 28
Future Shock, 72
Gartner, 75, 94, 96-97, 99
    Glossary, 108, 109, 110, 111
Gates, Bill, 30, 158
Gen-Xer(s), 3
global aging, 48-51
GlowCaps, 5
Godin, Seth, 107
Google, 9, 10, 21, 52-53, 60, 61, 63,
    71, 131, 139, 143, 147
    Docs, 76
    Earth, 64
    Glass, 53
    Ground Truth, 65-66
    Maps, 20, 30, 53, 64-69, 70, 71,
    76, 80, 81, 86, 158
    motto, 152
    Search, 3, 11, 27, 30, 137-139,
    140, 149-151
    Search bias, 150-151
    search engine, 9, 149
    self-driving car, 54-57, 62-63
    Street View, 66
governance, 127, 156-157, 159
grammar checker, 30
grandmaster(s), 43-44
Hadoop, 95
Haisch, Bernard, 112
Hanks, Tom, 123-124
Harris Interactive®, 5
Harris, Parker, 74
Harvard, 148
Harvey Jones, Sir John, 118

Hawking, Stephen, 29, 115, 158
hindsight, 104-105
Hiroshima, 159
HITL, *see* Human-in-the-Loop
Hitotsubashi University, 73
Hoar, Andy, 35
Holocaust, 159
homo interruptus, 2
Hoover, Herbert (US President),
    45-46
human potential, 4, 19, 20, 41-53
Human-in-the-Loop, 87, 156
iBeacon, 6
IBM, 9
    Deep Blue, 43
    PC, 42
    Watson, 9, 10, 122-123
IBM Research, 123
IDC, 94, 96-97
image recognition, 77
Implisit, 77
innovation, 1, 8, 9, 14, 17, 28, 29,
    33, 35, 36, 64, 72, 148
insight, 104-105, 107, 126
Insight Deficit, 4, 9
Insight Signal(s), *see also* Altify
    Max, Insight Signal(s), 109
Insight(s), *see also* Altify Max,
    Insight(s), 112-116
Intel, 41
intentionality, 51-52, 53
International Monetary Fund, 105
Internet, 5, 29, 131
    'minute', 1, 2
Internet of Things, 5, 76
    and Humans, 6
iPad, 93
iPhone, 67, 123-124

iPhoto, 93
IQ, 145
Jackson, Michael
    Beat It, 133
    Thriller, 133
Jagger, Mick, 139
Jobs, Steve, 15, 51
Johnnie Walker Blue Label, 5
JohnnyCab, 61
Kaizen, 114
Kalanick, Travis, 62-63
Kasparov, Gary, 43-44
Kassan, Peter, 42
Kay, Alan, 145
Kennedy, John F. (US President),
    46
Key Performance Indicators, 114
Keyhole, 65
Keynes, John Maynard, 45
Khosla, Vinod, 27
Kindle, 93
knowledge curve, 25, 47, 121, 122,
    130
knowledge domain, 11, 25, 60, 68,
    70, 81, 89, 97, 113, 120, 141, 142,
    154
knowledge economy, 18, 71, 72-73,
    126
knowledge worker(s), 7, 8, 10, 15,
    18, 19-21, 24-40, 47, 48, 52, 53,
    61, 67, 68, 69, 70-89, 91, 100,
    101, 103, 104, 113-114, 120-121,
    125, 126-127, 130, 137-141, 142,
    143, 144, 158
    future of, 19, 21, 40, 130
Laplace, Pierre-Simon, 16
Lean, 114
Leary, Adam, 98

Lenat, Douglas, 9
Lexus, 54
LinkedIn, 5, 13, 75
Louisiana State University, 33
Loungani, Prakash, *An Astonishing Record—of Complete Failure*, 105
Lyft, 69
machine bias, 153
Machine Learning, 18, 21, 36, 39, 48, 62, 77, 80, 81, 87, 90, 91, 123, 125, 127, 130-144, 146, 151
Machine Speed, 114
Machine Utilization, 114
MagicBand, 5-6
Manchester Derby, 125
Mansfield, Bob, 62
Marketresearch.com, 95
Massachusetts Institute of Technology, 46, 156
McAfee, 29
McAfee, Andrew, *The Second Machine Age*, 46-47
McFly, Marty, 104
McKinsey & Co, *Where Machines Could Replace Humans—and Where They Can't (Yet)*, 37, 38
Mechanical Turk, *see* Amazon, Mechanical Turk
Megginson, Leon C., 33
Mercury Project, 101
Metamind, 77
Microsoft, 9, 76
    Cortana, 9
    Office365, 75, 76
    Windows, 42-43
Microsoft Research, 157
Millenial(s), 3, 12, 15, 49
Miller Heiman, 80

Mimo, 5
MinHash, 77
Minsky, Marvin, 52, 119
MIT, *see* Massachusetts Institute of Technology
ML, *see* Machine Learning
mobile, 31, 65, 75, 77, 82, 100
Moellenhoff, Dave, 74
Moore, Gordon, 41
    Moore's Law, 7, 41, 42
Morgan, 122-123
multivariate statistics, 110
Musk, Elon, 29-30, 119, 158
Nagasaki, 159
NASA, 101
National Highway Traffic Safety Administration, 58, 60, 61
Natural Language Processing, 124
Navteq, 65
Nest, 6, 30
NHTSA, *see* National Highway Traffic Safety Administration
Nissan, 58
NLP, *see* Natural Language Processing
Nokia, 65
Nonaka, Ikujiro, 72-73
Notification(s), see Altify Max, Notification(s)
nuclear energy, 28-29
O'Reilly, Tim, 6
Obama administration, 58
Office365, 75, 76
open source, 6, 77
Oracle, 74
Orbison, Roy, *Pretty Woman*, 133
Otto, 63

Overall Equipment Effectiveness, 114
Page, Larry, 52, 53, 152
PageRank, 52
Palo Alto, CA
    Mayor of, 45-46
Pandora, 93
Perceptio, 62
Pew Research, *Public Predictions for the Future of Workforce Automation*, 38-39
Picasa, 93
Pitkäjärvi Lake, Finland, 66
Pokémon GO, 12
Polanyi, Michael, 47
Polanyi's Paradox, 47-48
predicting hit songs, 133-137
predicting recession, 105
PredictionIO, 77
Predictive Analytics, 4, 40, 76, 77, 80, 103, 108, 109, 110-111, 116, 118
predictive modeling, 110
Prescriptive Analytics, 4, 77, 103, 108, 109, 111, 118
Pretty Woman, 133
Prior Knowledge, 77
Process Speed, 114
Production against Target, 114
productivity, 11, 28, 31, 53, 71, 72, 73, 77, 79
ProPublica, 153-154
    Machine Bias, 153
Proverb, Croatian, 145
Public Predictions for the Future of Workforce Automation, 38-39
Quinn, Megan, 65-66
Quip, 75, 76

Rahwan, Iyad, 156
RDA, *see* Reciprocal Data Application
recidivism, 153-154
Reciprocal Data Application, 86, 87, 141, 143
regression analysis, 110
regulation, 159
Reject Ratio, 114
RelateIQ, 76, 77
relationship intelligence, 77
RFID, 5
robot(s), 20, 25, 27, 38-39, 121
    semi-autonomous, 40
    Three Laws of (Asimov), 25
Rolodex, 93
Rose, Axl, 139
Roundup of Analytics, Big Data & BI Forecasts and Market Estimates, 2016, 94-95
sales forecast(ing), 82, 83, 106
Sales Performance International, 80
Salesforce, 9, 20, 71, 73-79, 83, 86, 89, 99, 125
    AppExchange, 78
    Chatter, 86
    Einstein, 71, 78-79, 89, 125
    Opportunity Record, 86, 87
Samsung, 121
Sarbanes Oxley Act, 159
Satchidananda, Swami, *The Yoga Sutras*, 104
Scientific American, 51
Searle, John, 26
Selby, Dr. Louise, 152
self-driving car(s), *see* car(s), self-driving

self-parking car(s), *see* car(s), self-
     parking
seller(s), 14, 34-35, 81, 84, 86, 143
Senate (USA), 152-153
sentience, 25, 30, 32, 41, 130, 131
Sequoia Capital, 65
Silver, Nate, *The Signal and the
     Noise,* 9
Simon Rakov, Lucy, 101
Siri, 9, 30, 62, 123-125
SITL, *see* Society-in-the-Loop
Six Sigma, 114
Skynet, 26-27
Small Data, 81, 120, 139
smartphone(s), 2, 5, 6, 11, 12, 39,
     42, 60, 93
social media, 4, 17, 29, 35, 100
Society-in-the-Loop, 156-157, 158,
     160
Somme, 159
Spark Capital, 65
spelling checker, 30
Spotify, 93
SRI, *see* Stanford Research Institute
Stanford Research Institute, 52
Stanford University, 52
Steely Dan, 92-93
Stephen, Zackary, 44
stereotype(s), 152
strategy, 18, 126, 130, 142
Stratistics Market Research
     Consulting, 95, 96-97
Strickland, David, 61
Supervised Learning, 134-135
SXSW festival, 54, 61
Task Time, 114
Tele Atlas, 65
TempoAI, 77

Terminator, 27
Tesla, 58, 59, 61-62
The Automation Jobless, 46
The Death of the B2B Salesman, 34-35
*The Financial Times, An Astonishing
     Record—of Complete Failure,* 105
The Loud Hailer, 92
The Nightfly, 92
The Second Machine Age, 46-47
The Signal and the Noise, 9
The Yoga Sutras, 104
Thiel, Peter, *Zero to One: Notes on
     Startups, or How to Build the
     Future,* 102
think(ing) for a living, 15, 71-73,
     79, 91, 127
thinking, 7, 9, 12, 45, 50, 52, 53, 116,
     117, 127, 141
Thinking Chain, 116
Three Mile Island, 28-29
Thriller, 133
Thrun, Sebastian, 62-63
Thumb Generation, 3, 49
TIME, The Automation Jobless, 46
Toffler, Alvin, *Future Shock,* 72-73
TomTom, 65
Total Data, 95
Total Recall, 61
Toyota, 58
TQM, 114
training data, 48, 132, 134, 141, 142,
     160
trust, 114-116
Trust Quandary, 4
Turi, 62
Turing, Alan, 26
Tyler, Liv, 139
Tyler, Steven, 138-139

Uber, 30-31, 62-64, 69
University of California, Berkeley, 26
University of Manchester, 26
up-skill(ing), 28, 35, 48, 51, 122, 159
Urmson, Chris, 54-57, 60, 63
USA Today, 152
utility, 18, 33, 49, 91, 120, 160

value curve, 122
value-add, 18, 49, 121, 122, 126
venture capital, 80, 90, 98
virtual assistant(s), 125
visualization(s), 65, 102, 108
VocalIQ, 62
voice recognition system(s), 40
Waterville Golf Club, 67
Watson, 9, 10, 122-123
Waze, 65
Web 2.0, 6
WEF, *see* World Economic Forum
weighting, 135-136

WeMo, 6
Where Machines Could Replace Humans—and Where They Can't (Yet), 37
Where2 Technologies, 65
Why Are There Still So Many Jobs? The History and Future of Workplace Automation, 47
Wikibon, 94, 96-97
Wikipedia, 123-124
Windows, *see* Microsoft, Windows
Winograd, Terry, 52
Wirth, Nicholas, *Wirth's Law*, 42
World Economic Forum, 27-28
Yahoo, 65
Yardi, Ashwin, 122
Yellow Pages, 65
YouTube, 93
ZackS, 43-44
Zero to One: Notes on Startups, or How to Build the Future, 102
Zipdash, 65

OAK TREE PRESS

Oak Tree Press develops and delivers information, advice and resources for entrepreneurs and managers. It is Ireland's leading business book publisher, with an unrivalled reputation for quality titles across business, management, HR, law, marketing and enterprise topics. NuBooks is its ebooks-only imprint, publishing short, focused ebooks for busy entrepreneurs and managers.

In addition, Oak Tree Press occupies a unique position in start-up and small business support in Ireland through its standard-setting titles, as well as its training, mentoring and advisory services.

Oak Tree Press is comfortable across a range of communication media—print, web and training, focusing always on the effective communication of business information.

OAK TREE PRESS
E: info@oaktreepress.com
W: www.oaktreepress.com / www.SuccessStore.com.

CPSIA information can be obtained
at www.ICGtesting.com
Printed in the USA
LVOW04*1439041116
511686LV00013B/111/P